AT HOME WITH
white

AT HOME WITH
white

ATLANTA BARTLETT with words by **KARENA CALLEN**
photography by **Polly Wreford**

RYLAND
PETERS
& SMALL
LONDON NEW YORK

For Indigo, Hogarth,
and Bluey.

Designer **Pamela Daniels**
Senior editor **Miriam Hyslop**
Location research **Jess Walton**
Production **Sheila Smith**
Art director **Anne-Marie Bulat**
Publishing director **Alison Starling**

First published in 2007
This edition published in 2012
by Ryland Peters & Small
519 Broadway, 5th Floor
New York, NY 10012
and
20–21 Jockey's Fields
London WC1R 4BW

www.rylandpeters.com

10 9 8 7 6 5 4 3 2 1

ISBN: 978-1-84975-349-0

Printed in China

Library of Congress Cataloging-in-
Publication Data; a previous edition of
this book was cataloged as follows:
Bartlett, Atlanta.
  At home with white / Atlanta Bartlett;
with words by Karena Callen;
photography by Polly Wreford.
    p. cm.
  Includes index.
  ISBN: 978-1-84597-349-0
  1. White in interior decoration. I.
Callen, Karena. II. Wreford, Polly. III.
Title.
  NK2115.5.C6B375 2007
  747'.94--dc22
                    2006031489

A catalogue record for this book is
available from the British Library.

CONTENTS

There's an unfounded belief that white interiors are not for "real" people. For many, white exists only in the realms of rarefied coffee-table books, the pages of glossy highbrow design magazines, and in the icy cool of art galleries. After all, why would anyone who has muddy-pawed pets, furniture-clambering children with chocolate-smeared hands, or friends who all too often "forget" to take off their shoes and tramp mud through the house, contemplate decorating their home in the purest, most unforgiving of all the colors in the spectrum?

If you have been blinded to the wonders of white by the misconception that it is simply not practical, we hope that **At Home with White** will open your eyes. Practically speaking, washing machines, tumble dryers, cleansing agents, stain removers and washable paints mean that there's no excuse for avoiding white these days. And if white covers happen to get stained, relax—there's always bleach.

As for the notion that white is bland, soulless, and clinical, think again. White bestows an unmatched crisp, clean, and airy feel to any interior, regardless of where you are in the world—or what size your home happens to be. Not only that, it is timeless and will never date like other colors. You will never hear design or fashion aficionados say that any shade is the "new white" because it is always à la mode.

The perfect blank canvas, white offers limitless possibilities for collectors who love to display treasures and trinkets, from priceless antiques and artwork to thrift-shop finds and craft-market bargains. If that's not enough of a lure, white is indiscriminate and works just about anywhere, whether you live in an uptown apartment, a chic, city townhouse, a beachside bungalow, or a charming country cottage.

At Home with White is about how to make white work in your home. The key is to make sure that you introduce focal points and definition to avoid creating a "white-box." Using a variety of white shades—there are, quite literally, hundreds of colors to choose from—different surfaces and textures, accents of colors, and pattern can also prevent white from being bland.

We'll show you how to create a successful white interior that suits your lifestyle by giving you five inspirational looks to choose from. Classic White is both elegant and eclectic, marrying old with new to produce a sophisticated, grown-up interior. If you love the idea of escape, Romantic White will allow you to fulfill your fantasies by using chalky, pastel whites, theatrical touches, and sensual textures. For those who are drawn to the sea, Beach White shows you how to create a beach retreat wherever you live, with a blend of aquatic hues, rough wood, and beach finds. Country White is the epitome of easy, relaxed living for those who like an unfussy, simple home filled with comfort and coziness. Finally, discover the simple lines, calming neutral tones, and tailored upholstery that are the staples of Modern White, proving that contemporary does not equal austere. From there, we give you practical advice, stylish solutions, and foolproof tips to take white into every room in your home. If you ever had any doubts that white is the color for you, we hope that **At Home with White** will change your mind.

WHAT IS WHITE?

White has the appeal of the nothingness that
is before birth, of the world in the ice age.

WASSILY KANDINSKY

the spectrum of white

IN THE NATURAL WORLD, WHITE EXISTS IN UNDENIABLE ABUNDANCE. FROM THE SOFT, PEACHY WHITE OF A VOLUPTUOUS ROSE AND THE DELICATE, ALMOST TRANSLUCENT LEMONY WHITE OF A CABBAGE WHITE BUTTERFLY TO THE BLUISH WHITE OF FRESHLY FALLEN SNOW, IT IS RARE, IF NOT IMPOSSIBLE, TO FIND A WHITE THAT ISN'T TINGED WITH A TRACE OF ANOTHER COLOR.

The *Collins Dictionary* defines white as "the lightest possible color" and "the color of snow." It also explains that "white reflects more light than any other colored surface." It is this reflective quality, together with its purity and versatility, that draws us to white. Spilling over from nature into our homes, white, in all its manifestations, plays an increasingly pivotal role in 21st-century interiors. Pure, simple, cool, and serene, it possesses qualities that can transform an over-cluttered, chaotic living space into a tranquil oasis of calm.

So what is it that makes white so magical? Historically, white in its present form didn't exist until the invention of titanium dioxide in 1916, when brilliant white paint was born. Before that, natural ingredients such as milk protein, lime, and lead pigment had been used since antiquity, when they were combined to create muddy off-whites, a far cry from the clean, translucent whites that we have at our disposal today. Nonetheless, these ancient whites still exuded classical refinement. One of the most influential architects in history, Andrea Palladio, creator of the Venetian country houses that became known as villas in the late 1500s, used a distinguished palette

of off-whites and stone grays that are still referred to as Palladian shades. In 1782, a French chemist, Guyton de Morveau, created zinc oxide, a non-toxic pigment to replace the poisonous white lead previously used in paint manufacture. A further breakthrough came in 1916, when the Titanium Pigment Corporation of Niagara Falls, New York, and the Titan Co. AS of Norway began commercial production of a brand-new white pigment called titanium dioxide, which had a mid-tone that was neither warm nor cool. This purest of whites was adopted by the modernist movement and embraced by architects and designers such as Charles Rennie Mackintosh, Eliel Saarinen, Elsie de Wolfe, and Le Corbusier, who experimented with all-white color schemes. The English designer Syrie Maugham took white one step further in the 1930s when she introduced an opulence into white interiors that had not been seen before. Combining fur, feathers, and leather with mirrors, glass, and shells, she opened up white to a new audience. Since then, white has become synonymous with style, modernism, and simplicity.

Technically speaking, white isn't simply white. According to Sir Isaac Newton, what our eyes register as white is actually a combination of all the visible colors of the spectrum in equal proportions. Even pure white is rarely pure, since it has the chameleon-like tendency to take on a unique hue, depending on the colors around it and the light source, be it daylight or artificial light, so appearing pinkish, bluish, grayish, and so on.

What's more, modern paint manufacturers, having taken inspiration from the vast range of whites that nature has to offer, have concocted what seems like a neverending array of evocative white paint shades for us to lavish on our homes—white cloud, muslin, lime white, rosy white, bone, tallow, great white, Swedish white, flint, panel white—the list goes on. From chalky, cool, and creamy whites through to neutrals, gray whites, and muted whites, we are spoiled for choice. This array of whites has opened up limitless avenues of possibility for creating a variety of moods. Take a handful of creamy whites—buttermilk, white chocolate, and clotted cream—

and conjure up a relaxed, country feel or play with a palette of gray whites—stone, pebble, and dove gray—to give a room an Scandinavian feel. Provided you stay within the same harmonious color family, you can use white successfully throughout your home without it being bland.

As white not only changes with the light, but reflects it, it is indispensable in both urban and rural settings where natural light might be obscured by buildings or limited by small windows. It can bring luminosity to the dingiest basement or maximize brightness in a beamed cottage with low ceilings and leaded windows.

White is not as high maintenance and impractical as you might first think. Sticky fingerprints and muddy paw marks are easily removed from innovative wipe-clean paint surfaces, whether on walls or floors, and removable, washable slipcovers are the prerequisite of any family-friendly home. White is also compatible with contemporary lifestyle in a way that no other color spectrum can match. Inextricably linked to luxurious living, white has become the staple of modern, easy living. In addition to radiating light, white has the unmatched ability to maximize space. Small boxy rooms, and narrow corridors and hallways appear wider and airier when given the white treatment. In addition, it is a brilliant blank canvas for collections, artwork, heirlooms, and personal treasures, giving objects breathing space, hence the fact that it is the predominant color in galleries, museums, and department stores. The unique unifying quality it possesses means that it can be used to tie unrelated items together, such as furniture from different eras, which when painted white will sit together perfectly.

HOW TO USE WHITE

For those colors which you wish
to be beautiful, always first prepare
a pure white ground.

LEONARDO DA VINCI

texture

Texture is imperative in a white interior. Without it, everything blends into one, as our eyes are unable to distinguish between one object and the next—think "white cat in a snowstorm." At the turn of the 20th century, the Russian painter Kasimir Malevich highlighted the importance of using texture in his "white on white" paintings. He discovered that by using different types of white paint—oil, watercolor or distemper— he could express depth and dimension on a flat surface with just one color.

Using a variety of white shades within a room and introducing color accents can contribute to breaking up the flatness of white on white (more on this later) but it is texture that adds depth, dimension, and above all, definition. Light bouncing off a surface, be it a glossy white floor, a diaphanous white curtain, or a matt leather couch, creates a particular pattern of light and shade

that we not only recognize as texture, but also as color. That is why fabrics in exactly the same shade of white—such as flat cotton, satin damask, and fluffy terrycloth— can appear to be different colors.

Whether manmade or natural, we can gather textural inspiration from the world around us. The contrast of different materials makes each texture even more apparent. Think of the average cityscape, where luminous glass looks all the more beautiful against sturdy concrete, and how coarse brick brings out the grain in smooth wood. The same goes for nature. The sharp, jagged shape of a cactus is exaggerated against soft, desert sand. Why not take these textural influences into a white interior to bring it to life? On a country walk, collect everything from crunchy fallen leaves and broken twigs to downy feathers, and put them in glass frames or ceramic bowls to

embellish your homes. Even a trip to the hardware store can lead to the discovery of textural treasures, from a shiny zinc bucket and plastic laundry basket to balls of coarse garden string or a sisal doormat. Any of these elements placed in a clean, modern kitchen will give it a whole new feel.

The kind of textures that you choose will influence both the mood and the appearance of a room. Smooth, reflective objects and surfaces do double duty by boosting light and making spaces seem larger and airier. Porcelain cups and plates displayed on a rustic, country-style hutch are both a focal point and useful light reflectors, while a stainless-steel range brightens and updates a painted Shaker kitchen. Smooth surfaces are also a pleasure to touch. A limestone floor caresses bare feet; sandblasted glass feels almost velvety; and a soapstone bowl is a delight to handle.

You might not be consciously drawn to rough materials, but used in conjunction with other textures they serve a practical and aesthetic purpose within a home. Just think of seagrass or coir matting, which feels rough underfoot, is incredibly hardwearing, and makes a stark room feel instantly homey and welcoming. Similarly, pumice stone, sisal, and loofah not only bring a pleasing natural element into a crisp, clean bathroom, but also look divine when combined with the smoothness of wooden bowls and silky soaps.

You might not immediately think of a flat finish as being an important texture in a room, but when placed against glossy surfaces or objects, it plays a vital role. Matt marble floor tiles are the ideal contrast to polished-plaster walls. A high-shine injection-molded chair put next to a suede couch or a glossy wooden chair upholstered in felt will enhance both the shine and the flatness of the materials. Glass is also a marvelous textural device when employed to bring light into a dark corner or shadowy room. Cover a wall in different-size and shape mirrors, or have a piece of glass cut to size and then mount it on a bathroom wall to boost the light.

accents of color

Having a white interior is all very well, but not everyone wants to banish color completely from their lives. The good news is that you can introduce vibrancy into a predominantly white room with small explosions of color or one big, bold bang. Whether you opt for the subtle or the daring, the trick is to stick to one or two color accents that complement one another to make sure that the room still feels—and looks—white.

Color is a foolproof way of providing a focal point, one of the biggest challenges in an all-white interior. However, there is an element of strictness involved. If you want to highlight one wall with color, keep the other walls, ceiling, and woodwork white. You can go as bright as you like as long as the other elements in the room are white. If you are using a touch of color, such as soothing lavender in a bedroom or a sunny yellow in a kitchen, white woodwork will be a brilliant freshener, keeping the overall mood light and clean.

Although it is usually best to limit accents of color to walls, furnishings and finishing touches, floors can provide a vibrant shot of color. If you are bold enough to paint a floor vivid turquoise or pistachio green, keep everything else in the room white or off-white to prevent the color from taking over. A shocking Schiaparelli pink carpet laid in a gleaming alabaster white bedroom pays homage to old-style Hollywood glamour, creating fun and frivolity. A less daring but just as effective way to bring a splash of color is to jazz up white-painted floors with plain, colorful rugs in acid brights or pretty ice-cream colors, such as caramel, raspberry, and mango. The bonus of rugs is that they can be put away or discarded if you tire of the color.

Furnishings are another means by which color can be injected into the purest white environment to change the mood. A utilitarian indigo denim-covered sofa paired with white washed floorboards will give a room a relaxed, uncomplicated feel, while dark-chocolate-brown velvet will transform the same room into a luxurious comfort zone. Picking a single piece of iconic furniture will also bring a pop of color that attracts the eye and breaks up an all-white scheme. Take a vinyl-red molded plastic Verner Panton chair and place it in a cool white living room or a Pop Art-inspired Cassina Wink chair, which not only introduces color but is like a piece of sculpture.

Dark floors, such as fumed oak, mahogany, and iroko can also be used as an accent to white, reminiscent of Caribbean island interiors and colonial homes. Varnished and dark-stained floorboards will conjure up an effortless Balinese style, a great option if you have old floorboards that need a makeover.

As a rule of thumb, it is best to keep color to one or two areas or pieces of furniture and to avoid using too many shades. As with any rules, there are a few exceptions. Identical chairs painted in different candy shades will lift an all-white dining room without interrupting its purity. Likewise, painting cabinets powder blue in a white kitchen provides interest without spoiling the crisp, clean effect. Small hits of color work equally well to enliven a white interior. Throw pillows are a way to include color without making it overpowering—a cluster of scatter cushions in sorbet shades nestles beautifully on a white sofa. You can also use artwork and decorative objects to break up a block of white. A tropical-bright abstract painting or a collection of jewellike Murano glass can transform a monotone white living space.

mixing shades of white

Using white successfully in an interior relies on the subtle mixing and matching of different shades. You would be forgiven for thinking that all whites will work together, but in actual fact it's best to combine shades of white that come from the same color family.

Whites can be divided into six main color families: chalky, muted, neutrals, creamy, cool, and gray. Chalky whites include those ice-cream, pastel shades that are perfect for a romantic interior. Muted whites, on the other hand, work well in older homes and complement antiques beautifully, with their "knocked-back" subtlety. Neutrals, encompassing buff, taupe, and beige, have undertones of yellow, brown, or gray and work well in grown-up, elegant interiors. Creamy whites tend to be softer and warmer, are off-white tones that complement country settings. Cool whites have bluish undertones and lend

themselves best to very crisp, clean, modern interiors. Gray whites work well in cold daylight, hence their popularity in Scandinavian countries, and are a mix of black, red, and green pigments.

The first step in choosing the right color family for you is to decide upon the effect, or mood, that you want to create in your room and the furnishings and accessories you plan to use. You might have a Gustavian bedstead painted a beautiful pearl gray that is the focal point of a bedroom. Or your inspiration may come from a piece of postmodern furniture, such as a pure white Tulip table that will be best displayed against other cool white shades.

Don't hesitate to try out your chosen shades on walls, ceilings, and floor before you commit. White shades will look different depending on your light source, the reflection of other furnishings, and where you are in the world. Once you have decided

on the color family, you might want to consider how you are going to use the different shades. Painting walls, ceilings and woodwork, all the same shade will make them recede into the background, thus creating an ideal showcase for your furniture. Use white to play visual tricks in a room. Picking out woodwork and ceilings in a lighter shade than the walls will make a room appear taller and more elegant. Or paint furniture the same color as your walls, ceiling, and floor for a calming uniformity.

If you choose hues from the muted white family, try using a slightly darker shade on the walls and freshen it with a lighter tone on the woodwork. You can achieve a cozier effect in a room with floor-to-ceiling windows by painting the frames and ceiling in a dusky shade of buff to reduce their size and height, and the walls and skirting in palest mushroom white.

It's not just a matter of combining shades of white paint. Wood, furniture, curtains, and accessories all need to work together. If you want a white room that feels warm, choose creamy white accessories and a blonde oak floor. For more of a contrast, dark-fumed oak boards look striking against cool white walls and woodwork. A varnished chalky white stained floor teamed with delicate aqua-white walls give a room a laidback beach feel, especially in sunnier climes. Or you can choose a warmer, creamier tone that will still appear white but will be less stark than chalky or pure white in the northern hemisphere. Neutral toned flooring, such as seagrass, coir, and sisal matting create a calming environment when combined with taupe white walls and woodwork.

You can really let rip with white furnishings, filling a room with an abundance of textures and tones. Just remember to stay within the same color family of whites. If you have chosen a muted shade of antique white for your walls, cover your sofa in the palest parchment white. Or you might want to work with off-white or creamy shades, with buttermilk muslin curtains and armchairs in vanilla linen.

display

In an all-white interior, display allows you the opportunity to fully exploit a perfect, blank canvas. Not only does it serve a purpose by adding texture, accents of color and creating a focal point, it's another chance to customize your home. Almost anything can become decorative display. Family heirlooms, seashells and driftwood, vacation memorabilia, jewelry, enamelware, children's artwork, and old tin or vintage toys act as eye-catching punctuation against a white background.

But take note: display should not equal clutter, which is not only unfashionable but suffocating. What differentiates the two is the way that display is contained or structured within the constraints of a white interior, be it on shelves, in glass cabinets, clustered on the wall, or arranged on a side table.

Think carefully about what you want to showcase and how you want to exhibit it. A word of warning: you do have to be disciplined and stick to items that have something in common. Color-matching and grouping like with like will help you to weed out obsolete items. Try stacking a hutch with American creamware or line a shelf with a collection of pretty pastel-pale pitchers. Pairs of jewel-bright shoes lined up neatly on a glossy, white-painted floor and strings of beads hung on simple hooks on the bedroom wall turn everyday objects into out-of-the-ordinary artworks. A mantelpiece encrusted with an eclectic mix of plaster casts, antique Venetian mirrors, and fossils becomes a constant source of wonder. Common or garden objects like pots and pans, glass tumblers, mixing bowls, and gelatin molds grouped together and arranged symmetrically, or old mystery paperback-novels organized alphabetically on a shelf, take on a decorative identity.

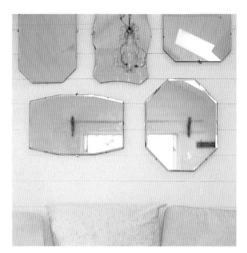

An incredibly beautiful singular object can also make a stunning focal point. A sparkling cut-glass candelabrum that catches the light will add a touch of glamour when displayed alone on a dining table. A gossamer-fine embroidered chiffon dress hung on a closet door gives a bedroom a boutique feel. A vast hand-carved wooden bowl picked up in a Moroccan bazaar and displayed in isolation on a low coffee table takes on a new distinctiveness.

Seek out interesting display cases and shelving. Open-fronted wooden cubes randomly stacked on top of each other are an inexpensive but effective way to exhibit crackleware ceramics. A tower of clear plastic storage boxes can hold trinkets and treasures that become *objets d'art* in their transparent cases. Even run-of-the-mill hardware-store wooden shelves can be revamped with a coat of eggshell paint to hold a carefully edited collection of china or ceramics in the kitchen or dining room.

When hanging pictures, discipline is essential. Pictures randomly dotted around a room lose their impact and will be far better hung in a group. Start by hanging the first picture at eye level and make it the center of the group, clustering the others around it. The same principle can be used to display different sizes and styles of vintage mirrors, old hats, or beaded handbags. Alternatively, you may want to create a more linear, art-gallery arrangement by propping a collection of framed black-and-white photographs against the floor and on rows of horizontal picture rails.

introducing pattern

Pattern exists all around us, and nature provides some of the most beautiful examples of pattern there are—the stripes of light and shade in a tree-lined avenue or the delicate veins on a fallen leaf. Such beauty can become a source of inspiration for our homes. You might draw from such patterns and cover a wall with a super-size leaf-embossed paper or introduce a sofa with ticking fabric.

In decorating terms, pattern can be used to enhance space and, to a degree, light. A subtle, faded-rosebud wallpaper can make a small room feel more spacious by creating fluidity. Vertical stripes on the walls will add height to a low-ceilinged room. A citrus-bright floral print used on one wall in a dark room can produce an illusion of sunlight.

Floors can be a surprisingly useful means of introducing pattern, without becoming suffocating. Brightly colored Mexican ceramic tiles will create a hacienda feel when paired with a roughly painted wooden kitchen and whitewashed plaster walls. A blue-and-white checkerboard wooden floor, inspired by colonial homes, looks eye-catching without being overpowering and will set off a country style perfectly. Even patterned carpets, which are currently experiencing a revival, can work in the right environment. With a nod to the aristocratic shabbiness of the faded floor coverings in British historic stately homes or turn-of-the-century hotels, subdued blossom and muted sprigs add another dimension to a pristine white interior, bringing luxury underfoot, and a welcome source of color and interest. Rugs, too, are enjoying a rebirth, with some of the most fashionable exponents including Cath Kidston, Lulu Guinness, Paul Smith, and Vivienne Westwood. Big blowsy peony prints, flags, jumbo-sized Damien Hirst-style spots, and Miro-esque abstracts can be thrown

onto brilliant-white floorboards or palest gray-white polished concrete to diffuse the starkness and to attract the eye. Intricately patterned handwoven kelims do double duty by bringing an exotic element to a living room or bedroom, while adding valuable warmth and vibrant color.

Furniture is another means of slipping pattern into a room without its dominating or compromising the whiteness. A chintz-covered, oversized sofa or an elegant pinstripe armchair look surprisingly at home—and contemporary—in all-white surroundings. Patterned bedheads make a decorative alternative to traditional carved wood or cast iron. An antique French bed with a headboard upholstered in chinoiserie embroidery looks decadent and sumptuous against a creamy white wall or, for a modern take on the same theme, opt for a tailored bed head with a striking floral print, a contrast to clean lines and minimalism.

Curtains and blinds can bring a measure of pattern into an interior in a contained way. A red-and-white gingham Roman shade makes a colorful addition to a pure white bedroom, adding country charm. Full-length, rose-printed curtains take the chill out of a white living room with high ceilings and huge windows.

Probably the easiest way to dabble with pattern in your home is with scatter cushions, throws, and accessories. Bright colored checked tablecloths, hand-embroidered vintage pillowcases, geometric patterned china, or a cool Andy Warhol Flower print can all look at home within a white interior. You can really use your imagination by playing with patterned accessories. In a country kitchen, a fashionably kitsch 1950s-style polka-dot oilcloth thrown over a chunky dining table adds a touch of humor, not to mention a blaze of color. A striped Mexican blanket picked up on your travels can transform a room when tossed over an old armchair or a couch. Small touches can make all the difference. Cover a lampshade with a bold-patterned wallpaper, frame scraps of vintage fabric, or hang a banner of embroidered crewelwork fabric on a wall. There's no end to the possibilities and pleasures that pattern can bring.

CREATING A MOOD WITH WHITE

Renoir said once that nothing was
so difficult, and at the same time so exciting,
to paint, as white on white.

AMBROISE VOLLARD

classic white

GROWN UP, ELEGANT, AND TIMELESS, A CLASSIC WHITE INTERIOR REQUIRES BOTH RESTRAINT AND SENSITIVITY TO TRULY SUCCEED.

OPPOSITE **A grand entrance hall combines the elegance of silver, gilt, marble, and wrought iron. The balustrade, salvaged from a reclamation yard, was made into a staircase by the owners. The stark white-painted floorboards and stairs are the perfect partners to delicate, pale gray walls. Reflected in the large mirror, a blackboard in a gilt frame adds a quirky touch to this hall.**

Think of a gentrified Regency drawing room, a Palladian villa, a charming French chateau, and you are on the right track. Everything has to possess elegance, and order is paramount. Quality presides over quantity. However, you don't have to slavishly recreate an historical scheme. Nobody wants to live in a museum, so feel free to incorporate your own unique and up-to-date spin on the classic theme. Mix refinery with witty details: a graceful 18th-century armchair with a slouchy, cotton slipcover or an oval Georgian-style table painted with porcelain-pale eggshell take on new identities more in keeping with the 21st century. Conversely, modern pieces of furniture can exude elegance. A high-backed, straight-sided couch with slender legs, a sleek aluminum floor lamp with a plastic shade, or a skeletal metal café table seem timeless within a symmetrical, well-dressed room.

Details are all important for this style to work. Use wallpaper and paneling to pertain to bygone days, juxtaposed with fresh white woodwork. Walls painted with understated colors and historically sourced paint shades will suggest past times effortlessly. Remember that brilliant white didn't exist until the 20th century, so the effect will be truer if you stick to shades that fall within the muted white and gray-white families. Original features, such as dado and picture rails, architrave, and ceiling moldings can be picked out in a lighter shade than the walls so they appear to fade away softly.

Offset ornate decor and antique furnishings with wide floorboards painted or stained white and varnished, smooth marble or travertine tiles, and herringbone-patterned parquet flooring.

These perennially fashionable floor treatments will not detract from the magnificence of a classic decorative scheme.

Fireplaces, whether original or a new addition, can bring a valuable focal point to the room. From sculptural stone and mottled marble to cast iron and ornate carved wood, the style of surround should echo the furniture and decor. A mantelpiece is just right to display collections, from vaporous glass candlesticks and treasured antiquities to a row of tiny votive candles and fragrant fresh flowers.

Bookcases or cupboards built into alcoves on either side of a fireplace, or a pair of Louis XV bergère armchairs facing one another in a window bay, bring a sense of balance to a room. Think about centering pictures, mirrors, and wall sconces rather than putting them up randomly. Symmetry also works well in a kitchen, with a range taking the central position and cabinets or drawer units on either side. Introduce an element of classicism with faux columns or pillars, which give the room, however small, a grandness that harks back to the high-ceilinged sculleries of country manors and chateaux. If you have the luxury of space, seek out gigantic double doors in an architectural reclamation yard and use them as dividers in the kitchen or living room.

ABOVE LEFT AND CENTER, AND OPPOSITE **Symmetry, coupled with elegant yet understated furnishings, gives this living room in a Victorian row a classical feel. A pair of French chairs have been rejuvenated with Ian Mankin gray-striped fabric. Throughout the room, shades of palest gray shift and change with the light to create a universal mood of calm. The chandelier illuminates and softens the look of the room. A gray marble fireplace displays flowers and candles, picking up the ornate carving on the mirror.**

ABOVE RIGHT **These cupboards were handmade from doors salvaged from an old French house.**

INSET **An apparently unrelated collection of candlesticks, 1920s picture frames, coral, and religious artefacts is pulled together by a cool white background on this mantelpiece. The carved relief plaque lends a further note of antiquity and reflects the pale plaster color of the walls.**

THIS PAGE **Flamboyant grandeur is introduced to a simple bedroom by this outsized carved headboard, cleverly adapted by the owners. Taupe walls bring an element of softness and warmth, tying in with a mink-colored velvet bedspread, while crisp, white bedlinen adds freshness to the look.**

When it comes to window treatments, paneled wooden shutters painted to match your walls and woodwork will inject splendor, while heavy drapes in beautiful antique fabrics not only look formal but will also add warmth and soften the edges of a room. Be aware that a classic white interior needs little in the way of excess adornment. Bookcases and side tables piled with books, old stone urns, a cluster of glassware, or a beautiful display of creamware china are enough to suggest faded grandeur and shabby sophistication.

romantic white

THERE'S NO BETTER BACKDROP FOR A SUCCESSFUL ROMANTIC INTERIOR THAN WHITE, WHICH BESTOWS JUST THE RIGHT AMOUNT OF MODERNITY TO A STYLE THAT CAN OTHERWISE VERGE DANGEROUSLY ON THE WRONG SIDE OF KITSCH.

In the past, romance was synonymous with overembellishment. Today, it is defined by a more pared-down sensuality that has little to do with frothy frills and all to do with curvy lines, glamorous touches, and the adventurous combination of vintage with modern and plain with pattern.

Romance comes in many guises, from fairytale to boudoir, and can therefore be adapted to suit a variety of tastes. It is not a look anchored in practicality, but a means of escape to whisk you away from the humdrum of everyday life. Put simply, romance is an antidote to the frenetic world in which we live. While there are no hard and fast rules to interpreting a romantic white theme, the key to keeping it contemporary and livable is to make it relaxed and pretty.

A palette of chalky, ice-cream whites is the perfect starting point. Pick whites with a hint of powdery blue, dusty pink, and faded lilac that radiate a flattering light conducive to a romantic atmosphere.

Nostalgia is the essence of romance, and patterned wallpaper or even fabric-covered walls can heighten the mood. Faded cottage-garden florals and rosebud prints, oriental sprigs of cherry blossom, and stylized Art Nouveau motifs all lend themselves naturally to the romantic room.

Extend the light touch to floors, keeping them pale and ethereal so that furniture "floats" on the surface. Bleached white Scandinavian-style-boards, white oak, bleached pine, and blonde maple planks reflect a celestial light that bounces off walls and furniture.

ABOVE **Mirrored sconces are brilliant for reflecting light. Here, a sconce has been embellished with a silk flower and a trailing garland of roses.**

OPPOSITE **A mix of antiques and 20th-century vintage pieces gives this girlish retreat a modern edge. An original antique French bed is both refined and glamorous with its intricate gilt detailing. Oriental touches, such as the bamboo table, cherry-blossom-patterned bedspread, and the jewelry box, are decidedly feminine. The owner has displayed a prized collection of silk flowers and jewelry on wire busts hung on the walls.**

ABOVE **A pretty, delicate rose-white Indian bowl with tiny rhinestones and a silver rim adds a soft girlish touch to a bedside table.**

ABOVE RIGHT **White and silver are used to maximum effect with an eclectic collection of ethnic accessories. Fur, silver, leather, sequins, and embroidery transform the plainest of living rooms into a heavenly sensory zone.**

OPPOSITE **This romantic interior has been created using a palette of whites, from delicate mushroom-white upholstery on the satin damask-covered seat to the palest dusty pink walls and off-white-painted furniture. The curvaceous chest of drawers is used to flaunt a collection of delicate glass, a crystal candelabrum, and white porcelain bowls.**

You can let your imagination run riot when furnishing a romantic interior. Don't shy away from theatrical or dramatic pieces and actively seek out furniture that tells a story or enhances a mood. Striking one-off pieces can really set the scene. An elegant carved wooden dresser painted in a subtle shade of mushroom white and bejeweled with glass-stoppered perfume bottles is reminiscent of a French boudoir. A mosquito net hung over an old iron day bed with peeling paint and decked out in crisp cotton pillows and bedlinen will suggest steamy nights in tropical hideaways, while an exotic Eastern banquette layered with multitextured throws and cushions transports you to a Moroccan medina. A mirrored Art Deco dressing table can become the centerpiece in a film-star-style bedroom. Fretwork and embroidered silk screens are both practical room dividers and playful props, creating a voyeuristic dressing-room vignette in the corner of a bedroom.

When it comes to windows, dress them up with filmy, gossamer, and diaphanous curtains and panels that will catch the breeze on a summer's evening. Transparent fabrics, such as lace and voile, will allow light to filter into the room but will keep out the sun's glare. Avoid anything overly frilly and flouncy that will turn the room into a parody rather than a paradise.

Banish the harshness of overhead lights, favoring instead the rosy glow of lamplight, the incandescence of flickering candles, and subdued daylight spilling through shutters or slipping in through sheer curtains. Small touches will make all the difference, so spend time on the finer points. Introduce a decadent decorative crystal-drop candelabrum to a bathroom. Layer sensual

THIS PAGE **An antique iron bedstead has been painted subtle dove gray, accentuating its intricate detailing. A utilitarian 1930s anglepoise lamp and a clean-line Arts and Crafts table prevent the room from becoming saccharine.**

OPPOSITE **A carved fretwork Indian screen has been given a new lease on life with a lick of duck-egg-blue paint. Not only does the screen provide a useful dressing area, but it also helps hide any undesirable clutter.**

fabrics such as velvet and satin, on top of one another to bring just a hint of sexiness to a bedroom. Hang a rose-tinted crystal chandelier for the ultimate in seductive lighting in a living room. Sequins, sparkles, and spangles come into their own in the romantic room. Use sequinned fabrics to make cushion covers, and beaded scarves or saris as throws and canopies. Pair blown-glass lamp bases with pearlescent paper or fabric shades. Prop your room with tantalizing treasures from past and present, home and abroad. The tease of a translucent vintage slip dress flung over a bedstead, pairs of bonbon-colored beaded slippers peeping out from behind an Indian screen, and strings of pearlescent beads piled extravagantly on a dressing table are subtly suggestive.

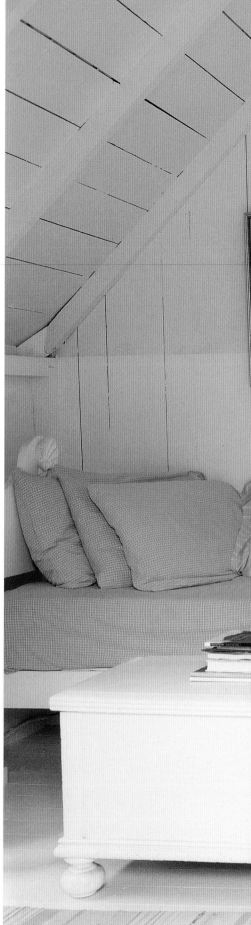

beach white

WHETHER YOU YEARN TO LIVE IN A
LUXURIOUS LONG ISLAND COASTAL
RETREAT, AN ENGLISH SEASIDE
HOME, OR A COZY NORTH-WOODS
CABIN, YOU DON'T HAVE TO LIVE
BY THE OCEAN TO ENJOY THE
PLEASURES OF BEACHSIDE STYLE.

A stormy winter's day can be just as
inspirational as blazing sunshine,
turquoise skies, and azure sea. You

THIS PICTURE AND OPPOSITE, ABOVE A Shelter Island beach house has been decked out in delicate stripes and shades of white and gray. A painted wooden bed with carved shell detailing doubles up as a sofa and a guest bed. The high vaulted ceilings have been scaled down by painting the upper half of the room gray, while the rest of the room and the furniture are all painted off-white.

OPPOSITE, BELOW Myriad shades of white can be found in this bowl full of pebbles and shells.

BELOW LEFT **A crumpled white linen sofa has a welcoming, lived-in look bedecked in beige-and-white striped pillows. Woven seagrass matting warms up the dark wooden floor.**

BELOW RIGHT **A cozy corner in a log cabin has been turned into an occasional work space, with an old kitchen table used as a desk. A vintage angle-poise lamp provides light when daylight fades.**

might want just a hint of beachside living to permeate your home. A monolithic driftwood sculpture, sun-bleached and weather-beaten floorboards, and shell-shaped door handles on a hand-painted chest of drawers will be enough to evoke a maritime mood.

For an all-out beach scheme, the right flooring is key. Take your pick from glossy, highly varnished boat decking that will reflect light and be an eye-catching contrast to oceanic white tones. Painted boards in eggshell blue, green, or lime-washed, look the part in a beach-themed room. You don't have to stick to wood. Concrete painted stark white works surprisingly well, lending an ultra-modern, Miami Beach feel, while cool marble tiles are reminiscent of the Italian Riviera.

Walls are another means of introducing seaside references into a room. Planked walls, either vertical or horizontal, are a failsafe way to create a beach-hut look. Visit a maritime supplier to find sailcloth and canvas, perfect

for making blinds or tab-top curtains. Simple Roman shades in creamy canvas sailcloth, nautical navy-and-white-striped cotton, or even sheer voiles work well, allowing you to let as much daylight in as you wish. Add to the seaside theme by buying cleats, eyelets, and pulleys from a maritime supplier in place of traditional fixtures. Echoing the vibrancy of English beach huts, cushions in candy stripes bring a refreshing splash of color to a cool white backdrop. Textural fabrics suit the mood. Soft, terrycloth-covered cushions in white, aqua, and cerulean blue are both practical and super-comfy, while white waffle cotton throws and pillows add instant freshness.

Beach life is synonymous with simplicity, so stick to fuss-free finishing touches. Authentic storm lanterns and lamps, naively carved wooden boats, pieces of rope, and lobster pots can be displayed simply on the wall or on rough, wooden shelves. The great thing about a beach-house interior is that it is achievable on the tightest of budgets—and with a minimum of effort.

BELOW LEFT **Pebbles and shells have been set into concrete to create a grotto effect on a beach-house fireplace. A row of books in muslin-colored dust jackets has been diligently organized by the owner.**

BELOW RIGHT **Yellow-and-white striped walls echo the lines of the tongue-and-groove paneling. Checkerboard linoleum tiles and a sheer curtain gathered on a simple wire lend a French feel to this beach retreat.**

THIS PAGE **Tongue-and-groove paneling is a sure way to suggest seaside living. A generous bunch of hydrangeas has been casually placed in a galvanized steel bucket and sits beside an old-fashioned fluted mixing bowl with a blue interior, adding texture and tone to the room.**

OPPOSITE **In this Scandinavian-inspired kitchen, a generously proportioned range sits comfortably with the painted furniture, floorboards, and kitchen units. The hutch-style wall cabinets with decorative brackets are shallower than standard units to make them more accessible. The sea-green Gripsholm table and Cape Cod chairs are both from Sasha Waddell. Daylight floods in through French doors, illuminating the room and accentuating the seaside feel.**

RIGHT **The owners of this Copenhagen home have turned an antique silversmith's workbench into an unusual side table. A collection of objets d'art is framed by a large ornate gilt mirror. A comfortable and handsome 18th-century Swedish chair gives a sense of scale to the adjacent grand dark wood bookcase.**

OPPOSITE **A color palette of white and naturals keeps this cozy space from becoming dark and "olde worlde." The fumed oak floors and black log-burning stove act as both anchors and accents of color. A large freestanding wood-framed mirror propped against the wall brightens up the room and a variety of woods brings texture and warmth. Decorative 1930s embroidered scatter cushions introduce country-style florals in a minimalist way.**

country white

COMBINE OFF-WHITES WITH NATURAL, EARTHY TONES TO PORTRAY THE PARED-DOWN PURITY OF SHAKER STYLE; BLUE- AND GREEN-TONED WHITES TO EXPRESS THE ELEGANCE OF SCANDINAVIAN COUNTRY HOMES; CONCRETE FLOORS WITH WHITE-WASHED WALLS TO PROJECT A MODERN COUNTRY MOOD.

Country style is ultimately about comfort, ease, and informality without harping back to the country look of the past with matching chintz and reproduction antiques. Primarily, it's about the honesty of the materials that you choose— wood paneling, raw plaster, hand-crafted furniture, natural fabrics— and about leaving out the superfluous and the overly ornate. Country style also focuses on living

THIS PAGE **This living room in an urban home is a prime example of "country in the city." The owner has used an array of whites to give the room a peaceful, relaxed feel. The furniture, a combination of Early American and Swedish styles, is the height of simplicity. The chair, from the Cape Cod range, and the Carl Larsson-inspired cot sofa are both by Sasha Waddell. A simple fireplace has been piled with logs to give the illusion of warmth.**

ABOVE AND LEFT **An idyllic summerhouse at the end of an English country garden provides a perfect retreat for the owners, while doubling as guest accommodation. A painted metal day bed is strewn with mismatched pillows for a playful take on country style. A crystal chandelier and 1940s mirrors add sparkle and glamour, contrasting with the bareness of the untreated floorboards. A pair of 1930s floral curtains and an old Aran sweater have been transformed into scatter cushion covers.**

OPPOSITE The union of bare beams and antique and vintage furnishing adds charm to this bedroom. A headboard covered in an embroidered 18th-century wall hanging looks modern because of its height. The 1950s floral sprigs on the wall and the delicate gilt chandelier bring a touch of prettiness. French grain sacks have been turned into pillowcases, a textural contrast to the cotton bedlinen and heavy handknitted blanket, which adds a cozy, comforting touch.

in harmony with nature, blurring the boundaries between outside and inside. A rough brick hearth might echo the outside walls, or flagstones from the garden patio could continue into the farmhouse-style kitchen.

White-painted tongue and groove gives walls a cozy feel; rough wooden planking yields a more rustic finish; unevenly plastered walls painted with distemper or limewash look authentic. If you are lucky enough to live in an older property, strip back the walls to reveal the original wallpaper or plaster, or peel back layers to uncover the beautiful patina of old paint for a deliberately neglected look. Sandblast woodwork to leave it bare or use a few layers of paint, sanding it to create a well-worn effect.

Like walls, flooring should look rugged rather than pristine and feel solid underfoot. Replace sleek, manufactured wooden flooring with wide, chunky floorboards; ditch neat ceramic tiles for reconstituted concrete; do away with carpet and use instead reclaimed flagstones, worn brick, or roughly woven rush or seagrass matting.

Country homes often have a quirkiness that comes from their owners being in tune with the simple pleasures of life and changing of the seasons. Furniture and accessories reflect this with a leaning toward comfy, hand-crafted pieces. Look for homemade cushions and hand-knitted blankets from craft markets and thrift shops. Buy a second-hand, slightly battered couch and make slipcovers of buttermilk linen. Pick up a wooden bench in a garden center and paint it with oil eggshell paint, sanding the edges to give it a distressed finish, or soften an Adirondack-style planked chair with cushions and use it as an indoor armchair. Sheepskins, rag rugs, and pure wool mats add warmth, color, and texture.

modern white

ABOVE LEFT AND OPPOSITE **Here,** a kitchen, dining room, and living room flow into one—the ultimate in open-plan living. The rawness of the concrete flooring is balanced by the organic presence of a log pile and the oak dining-room table and chairs. Tubular steel, felt, chunky knits, hand-crafted ceramics, and twinkling glass combine to make this a truly inviting space that appeals to the senses. The owners have hung a beautifully weather-worn metal panel on the wall to create a unique piece of art.

ABOVE RIGHT **Simple molded plastic garden chairs look at home against an edgy concrete floor.**

MODERNITY IS A MINDSET. IT'S NOT ABOUT HAVING GLASS WALLS, INDUSTRIAL FLOORING, AND HARD EDGES. NOR IS IT ACHIEVED BY BUYING A PHILIPPE STARCK LAMP, A JASPER MORRISON SOFA, OR A CHARLES EAMES CHAIR.

Modern is synonymous with simplicity, beautifully executed workmanship, and less rather than more—why have a dozen mediocre things when you can have just one beautifully hand-crafted vase or a gorgeous custommade sofa?

When we refer to modern white, the image that automatically springs to mind is the quintessential white cube that resembles an art gallery rather than a home. The origins of white are based in the modernist movement, where early exponents included Adolf Loos, the Bauhaus movement, and Le Corbusier. While it is true that there are 21st-century designers and architects who still gravitate toward minimalism and starkness when working with white, not all limit themselves to this view.

Nowadays, modern is not solely about strictness, but about the fusion of softness with severity, natural with manmade, and sharp corners with round curves. This equilibrium comes from counterbalancing materials. If you have huge floor-to-ceiling windows, make sure they are softened by the view of a beautiful garden or the sensuality of see-through voile curtains. Tame the sharp edges of

THIS PAGE **Vintage Hollywood** meets the 21st-century in this New York apartment. The 1930s chrome rocking chairs, picked up by the owner in Mexico, add fluidity to this formal seating arrangement. A tactile shaggy rug prevents the room from being too austere. Original black-and-white photographs by Peter Hujar, Lee Miller, Robert Mapplethorpe, and Dwights Michaels are displayed on picture shelves, allowing them to be easily rearranged. A verdant plant in the corner of the room and the striped pillows on the sofa add accents of color in this primarily monotone space.

an industrial concrete floor with the addition of natural raw materials, such as a sofa covered with a cashmere or mohair blanket or a pure wool rug.

Modern does not have to exclude links with the past, either. In fact, antiques take on a new splendor and sense of purpose in an unadorned, pure white space. A rusty metal chair, a beautiful lit bateau bed, or a Louis XV couch stand out all the more in a modern setting. In addition to contrasting old and new, hard and soft, natural and manmade, cleverly combining shades of white and using color accents can erase sharpness.

When planning your room, think about material partners that will enhance each other's qualities and uniqueness. If you are going to have a sleek, wood-strip floor, pair it with softer elements to stop your home from looking like a retail interior. Introduce textured walls, delicate soft furnishings and plump floor cushions in pretty shades of white. Or throw in an

OPPOSITE **Stainless steel** maximizes the impact of this minimalist, functional kitchen. The white walls and doors freshen up the otherwise industrial look.

RIGHT **An open-plan New York** kitchen and living area is neatly defined by the cast concrete and wood breakfast bar. Concrete has also been used for a slick work surface, a sharp contrast to the white-painted brickwork of the loft walls. Glossy, mirror-like floors echo the sheen of the stainless-steel wall units and appliances.

organic element, by lining an entire wall with stacked logs or honed wooden blocks. The new take on modern also relies on using materials in surprising new ways. Replacing traditional wooden baseboards with stainless steel is just one way of adding an unexpected twist to a white room.

Materials such as concrete are a modernist's gift, as they can be transformed in an almost alchemical way. From its rough-and-ready raw state, it can be polished to a glassy finish or mixed with pigment to change its color. Even mosaic tiles with their classical associations can become truly modern when made in metallic finishes, glass, or glossy white ceramics.

There are many ways to furnish a modern white home, from the obvious design classics, which are an effortless way to translate the look, or with an eclectic compilation of secondhand finds, antiques, and store-bought items. Contemporary classics have the added bonus of never dating and always retaining their value. A 1930s Rene Herbst tubular steel and rattan chaise longue looks at home on a raw concrete floor, while Philip Wolfson's grainy ebony cantilevered Prototype Desk sits well on a pure white-painted wood floor. Modern doesn't just translate to tubular steel, molded plastic, and slick wood. Unfussy upholstered furniture with clean, tight-fitting covers in plain materials and solid weaves fit the bill. Equally, a tatty 18th-century chaise longue with its original cover will look exceptionally avant-garde in a stark, white room.

LIVING WITH WHITE

White...is not a mere absence of colour;
it is a shining and affirmative thing,
as fierce as red, as definite as black...

G. K. CHESTERTON

living rooms

A LIVING ROOM SHOULD BE A PLACE TO UNWIND, KICK OFF YOUR
SHOES, AND LEAVE THE OUTSIDE WORLD BEHIND, EVEN IF IT'S JUST
FOR A FEW STOLEN MOMENTS. IT SHOULD BE A ROOM FOR LIVING,
WHERE YOU CAN FEED ALL YOUR SENSES AND ENJOY THE TOUCH
OF LUXURIOUS TEXTURES, THE TASTE OF VELVETY WINE, AND THE
VISUAL TREAT OF A FAVORITE PIECE OF ART. IT'S A MULTI-PURPOSE
SPACE WHERE YOU CAN DO ANY NUMBER OF THINGS, FROM
ENTERTAINING GUESTS TO SNUGGLING UP WITH LOVED ONES.
VERSATILITY AND COMFORT ARE THE MAIN PRIORITIES, FOLLOWED
SWIFTLY BY AESTHETICS. A PALETTE OF WHITES, OFF-WHITES,
NEUTRALS, OR NATURALS CAN ACHIEVE AN EASY, LAIDBACK
ATMOSPHERE IN A ROOM WHERE SO MUCH IS GOING ON. KEEPING
THINGS SIMPLE, AND CLUTTER OUT OF SIGHT, WILL ALLOW YOU TO
HAVE A REAL SANCTUARY FROM THE CHAOS OF DAY-TO-DAY LIVING.

LEFT The New York skyline, gently filtered by a translucent Roman shade, makes a striking contrast to this calm, elegant interior. The carefully considered blend of old and new furniture brings character and coziness.

OPPOSITE Soft tones of buff, taupe, and cream have been used to create a restful room in combination with the sensual mix of nubuck suede and velvet upholstery. Streamlined shelves set into the alcoves are the perfect place to display a carefully edited collection of books and treasures.

When creating a relaxing sanctuary or an elegant entertaining zone the backdrop is key. You might want flat-finish painted plaster walls or a highly polished marble-dust finish in an apartment where the living room is a retreat from hectic urban life. If you like to entertain in formal surroundings, subtly patterned wallpaper in muted tones of white makes for a grown-up look that is both sophisticated and sedate. Different types of panelling—from Georgian to Victorian—are also an effective way of creating a mood.

Much like kitchens, reception rooms tend to be exposed to constant traffic, so the practicality of flooring needs some thought. Wood flooring is not only warm and welcoming, but also a good choice for rooms that will undergo a lot of wear and tear. You can opt for pale woods that tie in with walls, woodwork, and furnishings, or make the floor the focus of a white room by using dark woods and stains. If you have old, beaten-up floorboards, why not paint the floor? Paint will hide a multitude

A cool interior pulls together a
collection of mismatched furniture.
The combination of all-white walls
and furnishings with the dark
wood of the oriental-style
mahogany table gives a colonial
feel. However, the eclectic mix
of furnishings—from the well-worn
Moroccan leather pouffe to the
elegant French-style side table,
showcasing creamware jugs and
a crystal chandelier—means the
mood is modern.

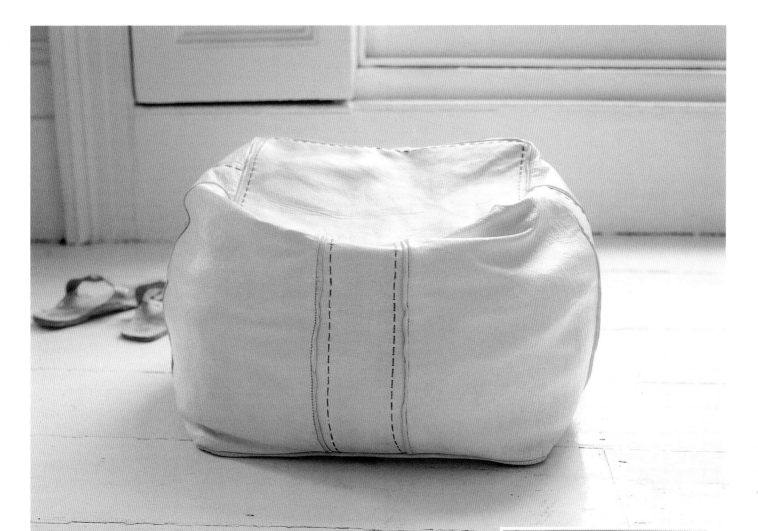

of sins, and again you can match the woodwork and walls to the color of the boards by having a specialized company mix it up for you. For living rooms with a country or Scandinavian feel, white stains can be used to create a lime-washed finish. You can also use a combination of lye, a type of bleach, and white soap, which acts as a sealant, creating a finish that evolves and improves with age. Floorboards can also be sanded and finished with white, clear, or dark oil to give them a subtle, satin finish.

One of the most important elements of designing your living room is the seating. A well-made, comfortable sofa is worth the investment. If you want to maximize space, choose a sofa on legs, which will make the room appear larger. A super-sized, squishy sofa covered in crumpled linen will lend a luxurious feel to the room, or

you may want to opt for the cleaner, sleeker, rectangular lines of a low-level white leather Citterio "Charles" couch. Space in a long, narrow room could be given definition by using a low-backed sofa as a room divider, ideal if you want to separate your eating and relaxing areas. If you have a wonderful view, position sofas and chairs to face the window, which will make the scenery part of the design scheme.

THIS PAGE AND OPPOSITE, BELOW
Natural tones of cocoa, mocha,
and café au lait soften the stark
whiteness of this period room.
A traditional sofa sits comfortably
on the bare white floorboards and
against hard edges of the concrete
coffee table. The curved lines of
the chair are complemented by the
organic texture of the shaggy
pouffe and the slender lines of the
white ceramics and triffidlike lamp.

OPPOSITE, ABOVE This old velvet
armchair, found in a secondhand
store, has been given a relaxed
feel by adding a sheepskin rug
and a faded floral pillow. The
mirror reflects light and brightens
up the room.

THIS PAGE **The owners of this Danish home made these banquette sofas from scaffolding planks and 1950s mattresses found in a flea market. The mishmash of striped cushions and retro lamps gives the room a bohemian look.**

RIGHT, FROM TOP TO BOTTOM **An Indian day bed turns an under-the-stairs nook into a cozy hideaway retreat. A prolific display of sculptural creamware emphasizes the graphic lines of black-and-white photos and artwork. In a seaside home a fumed-oak floor lends itself to a modern take on beach style. The inglenook fireplace, painted white, is decorated with pebbles strung on to a rope. A Victorian reproduction of a French bèrgere sofa is the focal point for this book-lined living room.**

In cities, where homes tend to be overlooked, curtains and blinds are more of a necessity than in an isolated rural location. Shutters are also an excellent option, as they provide insulation in colder weather, as well as privacy, and security. The clean, utilitarian lines of Venetian or wooden slatted blinds work well in any setting, a bonus if you have a south-facing room flooded by sunlight, as you can channel the light into the room by adjusting the slats. Roman shades provide a way to introduce texture, color, and pattern into a white room, since you can make them up in any fabric, from rough burlap, sheer cheesecloth, and vibrant silk to delicate faded floral or checked cotton. For an unadorned look, plain shades give you the option to have windows almost bare, allowing natural daylight to pour in.

For many, the soft drape of curtains is inextricably linked with a tranquil living space. From the formality and opulence of heavy, lined curtains to the relaxed airiness of gossamer gauze blowing in the breeze, curtains have a certain timeless elegance. You can introduce a pop of color with curtains—chartreuse linen drapes look eye-catching against a pure white wall, while deep-plum velvet will transform a pale, ethereal interior into a sumptuous retreat.

Keep lighting simple and directional by using floor and table lamps to create an ambience. In a period property, a decorative chandelier with a dimmer switch and reduced-wattage bulbs can

ABOVE LEFT **An open stairwell with a tension-wire handrail creates a gallery feel.**

ABOVE RIGHT **The owners of this New York loft have captured a Mediterranean mood by using antique and modern pieces against an all-white background on slick, wooden floors.**

OPPOSITE **Here, industrial chic combines with modern classics. The luxurious velvet "Charles" sofa, from B & B Italia, and the dark wooden floor bring accents of color to the monotone scheme. The S-shaped cocktail table by Piero Lissoni provides useful storage.**

introduce soft overhead light when you are entertaining.

There's nothing more welcoming in a living space than a blazing fire, whether in an original Victorian grate surrounded by a marble or carved wood fireplace or in a modernist niche. If you haven't inherited one, search in salvage yards and antique markets and get a builder to fit it for you. Even if a chimney has been blocked up long ago, it doesn't take much effort to reopen it. Wood-burning stoves create instant coziness too. An

ultra-modern stainless-steel stove can look amazing suspended in an open-plan loft living space or a restored barn. Traditional wood-burners are now available in a choice of colors, including white, and look perfect in a country-style living room or coastal interior.

And, finally, remember to keep your living room clutter-free in order for it to remain a restful zone. Streamlined, built-in storage cupboards can be used to house TVs, DVDs, toys, books, and electrical equipment.

ABOVE An air of rural ease pervades this room. Softness comes from the slipcovers, faded floral cushions, and delicate wrought-iron tables; while the imposing paneled fire surround draws attention to the simple fireplace.

OPPOSITE, BELOW LEFT **Banquette-**style sofas and linear modern furniture contrast with a carved wooden mirror and an ancient-looking urn.

OPPOSITE, BELOW RIGHT **A pair of** marshmallow, oversized armchairs add a soft touch to this elegant paneled room with its high ceilings and imposing staircase.

RIGHT **A cozy corner in a country** home is given a feeling of space and light with the addition of a large, framed mirror. Snuggly sheepskin, cable knits, and faded floral cushions in creamy tones add a homey feel.

kitchens & dining rooms

NO MATTER WHERE YOU GO IN THE WORLD, THE KITCHEN IS AT THE CORE OF EVERY FAMILY HOME. A PLACE FOR NURTURING, NOURISHING, AND CULINARY CREATIVITY, IT'S WHERE WE FEED BOTH BODY AND SOUL. WITH OPEN-PLAN LIVING BECOMING THE NORM, KITCHENS PLAY AN INCREASINGLY IMPORTANT ROLE IN OUR LIVES. NO LONGER SOLELY FOR THE PREPARATION AND DISHING UP OF FOOD, KITCHENS ARE A PLACE FOR ENTERTAINING, FOR FAMILY AND FRIENDS TO CONGREGATE, AND FOR RELAXATION. IN MODERN HOMES, DINING ROOMS AND KITCHENS TEND TO BE AMALGAMATED INTO ONE MULTIPURPOSE ZONE, SINCE FEW PEOPLE HAVE THE SPACE OR THE INCLINATION FOR A SEPARATE EATING AREA. AS IT IS THE HUB OF YOUR HOUSE AND OFTEN THE FIRST PORT OF CALL FOR VISITORS, IT NEEDS TO BE AESTHETICALLY PLEASING, AS IT IS A SHOWCASE FOR YOUR PERSONAL STYLE.

Storage units are an essential part of any kitchen. Not only do they represent a hefty financial investment, they will form the basis of the room for years to come. Avoid recreating a kitchen showroom by putting your own stamp on the design and combining contrasting textures, such as wood with stainless steel, glass with white lacquer, or stone with laminate. Mix open shelves with cupboards and cubbyhole storage with freestanding furniture.

Don't feel you have to conform to a stereotypical built-in kitchen plan—think carefully about what you need in order for your kitchen to run smoothly. And take time to define the mood you want to create. Do you want a slick, industrial space or an unpretentious Shaker-style country kitchen, a Parisian café look, or a retro 1950s-style diner?

Dare to mix past with present, old with new. A robust ceramic sink set into an old workbench adds an element of surprise in an otherwise built-in

OPPOSITE **A grand-scale kitchen in a New York loft has more in common with the scullery of a French chateau than a modern urban apartment.**

ABOVE LEFT **Here, floor-to-ceiling windows are softened by gauzy sheer curtains. A chunky dining table is teamed with elegantly upholstered chairs, creating a comfortable zone for entertaining and socializing.**

ABOVE RIGHT **Oversized pieces of china help balance the high ceilings.**

RIGHT **A Scandinavian-style round table with matching stools is both utilitarian and practical in a family kitchen.**

FAR RIGHT AND OPPOSITE **Shades of white and palest gray keep the rustic elements of this small kitchen from looking too countrified. Space-saving folding garden chairs, paired with a chunky wooden table, create a focal point. Simplicity is maintained by floor-to-ceiling cabinets housing kitchen paraphernalia. A simple sink unit with a monoblock faucet is ideally positioned by a large window, where light floods in unhindered.**

BELOW **Snow-white iced cupcakes on a glass cake stand are the epitome of purity.**

kitchen while a baby-blue 1950s glass-fronted hutch with a flip-down work surface is a whimsical addition to any culinary space.

Work surfaces are a vital part of your kitchen. They need to be hard-wearing and easy to clean as well as being good-looking. Wooden counters are always a popular choice, although they will need to be oiled regularly and sanded from time to time. Chunky maple, birch, and beech work well in a predominantly white kitchen and fit harmoniously with stainless steel, painted cabinets and glossy finishes. Or you might want to contrast white cupboards, walls, and floors with dark wood surfaces, such as iroko and wenge, both of which fare well in kitchen conditions. Marble, whether honed to create a matt surface or highly polished,

silvery gray granite and cast concrete are all durable and easy to maintain, as well as being elegant. Laminated countertops, which had fallen out of fashion until recently, are practical and aesthetically desirable. They come in myriad whites and creams, as well as pastels and bolder hues, that can all be matched to paint colors, allowing you to tie in the color of walls and cabinets to your countertop. If you prefer a rough, rustic finish, wooden flooring planks make a textural change to sleek, shiny counters. Paint them white, or sand and oil them, both of which will sit comfortably in a country-style kitchen.

A stove is another vital investment. You might build a kitchen around a much-used heavy-duty range, such as a Viking or

THIS PAGE The combination of stainless steel and high-gloss white lacquer gives this kitchen a glamorous, ultra-modern look. Although linear in design, the clever mix of textures and shades of white lends a soft, feminine feel.

OPPOSITE White creates a feeling of spaciousness in a small galley kitchen. The cabinets are the perfect foil for the aqua glass counters, which also inject a hint of soothing color. Huge glass doors open onto a beautiful planted patio.

THIS PAGE **This kitchen is the hub of an English country home. A 12-foot dining table, complete with its original distressed paint finish, is paired with practical seating. The hutch is used to display china and a collection of glass cake stands.**

OPPOSITE **In this barn-style kitchen, benches provide casual seating. Painted concrete floors care practical and economical. Hand-painted price cards from an old tea warehouse are displayed in simple white-painted frames.**

Wolff, or opt for a shimmering stainless-steel stove. Reconditioned or reproduction enameled 1950s stoves can look stunning in a modern setting. The same goes for refrigerators, which have become design statements in themselves. From the massive proportions of a double-door refrigerator freezer and the pastel prettiness of a Smeg retro model, to built-in fridge-freezers tucked secretly away, your choice is a matter of taste and space.

Don't neglect the smaller details when designing your dream kitchen. Everything down to the handles on your cabinet doors needs

to be both practical and pleasing to the eye. From shiny chrome and galvanized steel to carved wood and retro enamel, handles come in a huge array of finishes and shapes. Concealed touch latches or drilled holes are good alternatives if you want to keep your units streamlined.

Unless you favor ultra-minimalist decor and plan to keep all your utensils, dishes, and glassware, hidden in drawers and cupboards, kitchen shelves and hutches provide the perfect opportunity for display.

A painted Welsh hutch is the ideal backdrop for collections of chintz china, vintage enamelware, or delicate glass cake stands and domes. Don't be blind to the beauty of everyday objects, such as Duralex glasses and piles of white plates displayed en masse on a trolley, open shelf, or glass-fronted cupboard. The same goes for flatware, which can look anything but ordinary when placed in bundles in glass pitchers or large glasses.

A dining area needn't be complicated to create. An alcove can house banquette seating with a central diner-style table, especially useful for families and casual entertaining. A rustic refectory table with long benches for seating in the center of the kitchen will make a big impact if you have the room. Round tables are the best option for socializing and gathering around, while glass-topped tables, although high-maintenance and not child-friendly, maximize light and space.

BELOW LEFT **The white tongue-and-groove paneling and wooden window shutters take the edge off the metal fixtures in this kitchen. Open glass shelves are used to display sparkling glassware.**

BELOW RIGHT **Massive sliding doors allow light to illuminate this dining area, connected to the adjacent kitchen by a large serving hatch. Ultra-modern chrome and white furniture contrasts with the romantic femininity of the crystal candelabrum.**

OPPOSITE, LEFT **White laminated cabinets, stainless-steel appliances, and wooden counters are balanced by more traditional tongue-and-groove paneling and a fumed oak floor. Old school stools offer practical seating at a breakfast bar.**

OPPOSITE, RIGHT **A striking combination of black and white is accented by red glassware the owner bought in Camden Market, London. He also designed the streamlined kitchen, with its sleek minimalist lines and bold color combination.**

THIS PAGE **An open-plan living and dining area feels light and spacious, continuing into the garden beyond. A table, made from large slabs of oak, offsets the organic, curved lines of the wood-slat and chrome chairs. A pile of logs set into the alcove in the wall ties in with the wooden furniture, adding an element of warmth and coziness to this hard-edged interior.**

ABOVE LEFT AND RIGHT **In this Danish home free-standing, industrial units and appliances create a functional and stylish kitchen. The addition of vintage accessories makes it homey, while the light from the old window salvaged from a warehouse provides subtle illumination.**

OPPOSITE **Bric-a-brac adds quirkiness to this spacious country kitchen. White paint unifies the freestanding furniture and units.**

OPPOSITE, INSET **An eclectic collection of old tiles, china, and coffee containers.**

Wicker and chrome chairs teamed with a rough-hewn country kitchen table are a relaxed combinations while folding slatted garden chairs offer a casual dining option. An island unit or breakfast bar with slender wooden stools is perfect for ad hoc dining. For a Scandinavian flavor, Gustavian carvers with faded floral or checked upholstery are elegant in a more classical dining area. You could also bring in a splash of color with Arne Jacobsen's "Ant" chairs painted in varying shades of white or ice-cream pastels.

It's not difficult to dress up your kitchen for entertaining. Replace your day-to-day oilcloth with bleached-white linen and a mass of votive candles in glass jars. Scour yard sales and flea markets for old linen napkins, which you can hand-dye in beautiful shades to complement or contrast with your tablecloth. Make a simple but elegant floral display by arranging bunches of roses or full-blown peonies in glass fish-bowl vases or rustic galvanized buckets. The secret is to make it look effortless.

bedrooms

OF ALL THE ROOMS IN YOUR HOME, THE BEDROOM SHOULD BE YOUR
PERSONAL SANCTUARY. NOT ONLY IS IT A PLACE TO FULFILL YOUR
FANTASIES, DECORATING OR OTHERWISE, IT IS ALSO THE ULTIMATE
RETREAT FROM THE MAYHEM OF EVERYDAY LIFE, A PEACEFUL PLACE
WHERE YOU CAN DREAM AND, OF COURSE, SLUMBER COMFORTABLY.
NO SHADE IS AS SOPORIFIC OR SEDATIVE AS WHITE, MAKING IT THE
IDEAL COLOR FOR BEDROOMS. RESTFUL ON THE EYE, CALMING
TO THE PSYCHE AND A NEUTRAL BACKDROP FOR YOUR TREASURED
POSSESSIONS. PERSONALIZE YOUR PARADISE BY DISPLAYING
FAVORITE PIECES OF JEWELRY. DELICATELY ENGRAVED MOROCCAN
TEA GLASSES OR SIMPLE GLASS TUMBLERS LOOK ALL THE MORE
BEAUTIFUL FILLED WITH BEADS, NECKLACES, AND BRACELETS.
LOOK FOR CARVED WALL BRACKETS AND ENAMEL SCONCES
TO USE FOR DISPLAYING JEWELRY AND ACCESSORIES.

OPPOSITE **This pretty interior in a Victorian house is the epitome of pared-down luxury. The antique French bed, with its intricately carved headboard, has been painted creamy white, while a wooden chair doubles as a quirky bedside table on which to display a crystal and metalwork lamp. Generous continental pillows lend a luxurious touch, complementing the soft, lilac floral cushions and the delicate lace-edged duvet.**

White doesn't have to be cold. Warm up white with touches of texture, color, and pattern. With texture, mix and match fabrics and materials that might not normally sit together. Team chunky knits with gauzy voile, contrast carved wood with tactile velvet, or flaunt sparkly sequins alongside daintily embroidered quilting. Color will also boost warmth in an all-white bedroom, whether you opt for the palest sorbet shades, chalky pastels, or a pop of vibrant color. Peppering a bedroom with pattern makes it feel more personal, be it with a subtle floral vintage wallpaper, a dazzling tropical bedspread, or a bold digital-print wall hanging.

As a general rule, walls that are light and soothing will be conducive to rest and relaxation. Paint them in soft, muted shades such as ivory, pearl, or oyster to keep the look understated. You might decide to pick out one feature wall, perhaps behind your bed, with wallpaper. Soft, fluid designs such as those by Neisha Crosland, florals and rosebuds by Cath Kidston, classic, hand-blocked designs by Colefax & Fowler, exotic Eastern patterns and magnolias by Cole & Son, or historically inspired prints from Farrow & Ball—all work beautifully against predominantly white walls, woodwork, and ceilings. Reworked classics, such as Maija Isola's Unikko flower, 1950s polka dots, and psychedelic 1960s-swirls can work in small doses in an ultra-modern bedroom. You don't have to spend a fortune. Search for rolls of vintage wallpaper in thrift stores, on Ebay, and from companies on the internet—one or two rolls can be enough to cover a wall and to make a stylish, unique statement.

By comparison to other rooms, there is much less traffic in a bedroom, so you can choose more

RIGHT **A gossamer silk rose in a gold-rimmed teacup picks up the muted pattern of the wallpaper.**

OPPOSITE **Neisha Crosland wallpaper softens the lines of this small room. Shades of white, gray and silver work together to create a cool, calming bedroom that is romantic and indulgent. An antique French headboard is painted to match the floorboards. Textural touches such as the smooth gray marble top on the chest of drawers, the quilted silk bedspread, the glass lamp stand, and the decorative picture frames add glamour, while the shutters on the windows keep the look down-to-earth.**

delicate finishes. Pale wood floors and painted boards are warm underfoot, while a buff or off-white pure wool carpet instills a sense of five-star luxury. Limestone flooring will create a Mediterranean feel, especially if you splash out on underfloor heating, or you can add warmth with scatter rugs.

Ultimately, a bedroom is a place to sleep, so a comfortable bed should be your priority. The centerpiece of the room, the style of bed you choose will set the tone, whether you go for a sleek, modern steel frame or an original Victorian cast-iron bedstead. A French upholstered bed with the original fabric looks all the better for its tattiness, creating an air of shabby splendor. If the fabric is beyond repair, remove the upholstery to leave the ornate carved frame, which can look incredibly avant-garde in a pared-down white setting. A traditional four-poster bed design recreated in tubular or galvanized steel looks equally stunning in an industrial loft or a rustic interior. For tailored elegance, a padded headboard with a removable fabric cover in waffle cotton, antique linen, or heavy-duty canvas for easy washing, is fresh and contemporary. Add ties or buttons to create interesting detail. For a more spartan effect, opt for a divan bed with no headboard and place it against a paneling or planked wall, adding generous continental pillows for support while you are reading.

A bedroom has to be practical, too. It's a place to house your clothes, shoes and books, not to mention prized possessions such

ABOVE **An old chest of drawers has been rejuvenated with a coat of paint. A decorative shelf provides ample storage for jewelry boxes and glass jars full of ornamental hairclips. Hooks below the shelf provide a practical and unusual way to display necklaces.**

as jewelry, collectable trinkets, and family heirlooms, so storage is essential. In an urban home, original Victorian built-in cupboards can be restored to offer ample wardrobe space, while nooks and crannies above are the ideal spot for storage boxes. Alternatively, have a local carpenter build a closet wall, disguising the doors with tongue-and-groove, paneling, or plain composite board with touch latches inside.

An organized closet or large cupboard, whether built-in or free-standing, is a boon. Stack clear shoe boxes at the bottom, put hooks on the inside of the doors to

hang belts, scarves, and ties, and add a hanging rod across the width of the closet to give you enough space for dresses, shirts, skirts, and coats. Underwear, socks, and T-shirts are best tucked away in a chest of drawers, on individual shelves, or in baskets. Scour thrift stores for old dressers, chests of drawers, blanket chests, and bookcases, which can be painted white to so that, whatever era they are from, they sit well together. Old department-store-style chests with glass drawer fronts make excellent storage units. Find them in antique stores or check out furniture stores such as Habitat and Ikea for modern

THIS PAGE **A simple frameless mirror stands casually propped against the wall. A 1940s floral dress and a 1930s beaded evening top become pieces of art hanging on decorative hooks.**

OPPOSITE, TOP LEFT **A Victorian armchair is given a new lease on life with a crumpled linen slipcover. A simple wooden shelf holds books that have been neatly ordered.**

OPPOSITE, TOP RIGHT **A pull-down bed is concealed in an alcove to provide guest accommodation in this modern, urban home. The pure white walls, tiled floor, and huge windows are softened by the view of a blossom tree in the courtyard garden beyond.**

versions. Linen presses and armoires, either original or reproduction, are also worth hunting down for their generous proportions and flexible storage possibilities.

A bedroom should be a private, intimate place, shielded from the harsh glare of the real world. Transparent fabrics, such as fine linen, organza, and voile, make perfect curtains, allowing light to seep in seductively. Hang them on rods that tie in with your bed frame, such as tubular steel or painted wood. Antique lace panels can be hung in place of traditional curtains, with a simple roll-up shade behind for extra seclusion. Wooden shutters can be adapted by drilling tiny holes in intricate patterns similar to 1950s larder fronts to allow pinpricks of light through, and opaque clear plastic shutters will diffuse light and protect privacy while keeping the room bright.

No bedroom should be without a mirror, unless you are lucky enough to have an adjacent dressing room. Not only are mirrors vital when you are getting dressed or doing your make-up, they are also invaluable light reflectors and enhance the sensual mood of a bedroom. Prop an oversized decorative mirror against a wall for a decadent look or mount one on a wall in a rough, reclaimed wooden frame in a beach-style room. Full-length mirrors on stands are a flexible option since they can be moved where and when the mood takes you.

Lamps and lighting are of paramount importance in a bedroom. If you love reading in bed, make sure you have a bedside lamp that you can easily reach. Central lighting should be on a dimmer switch to allow you to soften the light, as there is nothing worse than harsh, bright lights in a bedroom. If you are creating a romantic room, chandeliers are instantly evocative. From

LEFT **A book lover's dream bedroom in a tiny New York city apartment. The bare simplicity of this near-monastical room is tempered by the friendliness of** the books piled on a bedside table and stacked willy-nilly on the shelves. Venetian blinds allow light to filter through, while affording much-needed privacy.

BELOW **A decorative cupboard provides storage in a seaside bedroom. To bring the outdoors inside, the owner has used an old wire garden chair as a jardiniere for trailing ivy.**

RIGHT **An iron bedstead has been partially painted white to create a decorative effect in this plain, country-style bedroom.**

FAR RIGHT AND OPPOSITE **A reclaimed window has been fitted in a hallway to create a vista through to the bedroom from the stairwell in this Copenhagen home. A simple divan bed on industrial castors acts as a sharp contrast to the period features in this bedroom.**

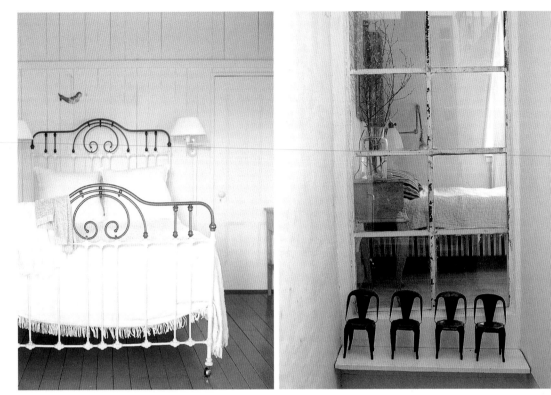

antique crystal to brightly colored modern glass, find one that suits your decorative style. Fairy lights also look beautiful all year round woven around a bedstead draped over a mirror or along a mantelpiece.

Dress your bed to set the scene. You might want to give your room a seasonal makeover by having summer and winter bedlinen. For the warmer weather, introduce seersucker and crisp cotton duvets and throws,

keeping blankets close at hand if it gets chilly. Swap to cozy, jumbo-stitch knitted blankets and handmade quilts during the winter months, teaming them with flannel sheets if you live in a very cold climate. Stick to cotton and linen sheets whatever the season, since their natural fibers let your skin breathe and keep you cool. If you feel nurtured and cocooned, you will be more likely to get a perfect night's sleep.

LEFT The mood is Zenlike in this pared-down bedroom. Bare walls, stripped and painted floorboards, and custommade clear plastic shutters create a fuss-free environment. Spartan metal furniture, such as the bedstead and side table, have a modern elegance, while the chunky reconditioned Victorian radiator has a nostalgic feel. Welcome softness comes in the form of a luxurious chunky knitted bedspread, while a simple flower arrangement adds a touch of femininity.

bathrooms

FOR CENTURIES, DIFFERENT CULTURES HAVE CONSIDERED
WASHING AND CLEANSING TO BE NOT ONLY A DAILY ABLUTION BUT
ALSO CEREMONIAL AND THERAPEUTIC RITUALS. FROM COMMUNAL
ROMAN BATHS TO SWEDISH SAUNAS AND HOT TUBS, BATHING AND
WATER SIGNIFY BOTH A SOCIAL AND A PURIFYING PROCESS AROUND
THE WORLD. IN THE MODERN WESTERN WORLD, BATHROOMS ARE
A RELATIVELY NEW PHENOMENON, ONLY REALLY TAKING OFF IN THE
EARLY PART OF THE LAST CENTURY, WHEN BATHROOMS BECAME
PART OF THE AVERAGE HOME, AS OPPOSED TO BEING SOLEY THE
POSSESSION OF THE RICH. NOWADAYS WE LOOK AT OUR BATHROOMS
AS LITTLE HAVENS OF LUXURY. THE BATHROOM IS A PLACE FOR
CLEANSING BOTH BODY AND MIND—AN INTIMATE OASIS OF SELF-
INDULGENCE FOR WHICH WHITE, WITH ITS INHERENT QUALITIES OF
PEACE AND TRANQUILITY, IS THE PERFECT BACKDROP.

RIGHT Simple but decorative paneling has been used to give the high-ceilinged room a cozy feel. An antique French café table is the perfect place for collections of shells, toiletries, and flowers. Pretty floral teacups on the window ledge store soap alongside old glass jars and bath oils.

Roll-top bathtubs, inevitably, take up a lot of room, but for most of us they offer the ultimate in luxurious bathing. Cheaper, space-saving acrylic or enameled tin tubs can be fitted neatly against a wall or in a corner and can be housed behind paneling or tiles. You don't have to be swayed by conventionality. These days you can take your pick from beautiful Japanese-style cedar tubs, which smell wonderfully aromatic and feel warm to the touch, or a reconstituted stone bath, which not only looks monolithic but is incredibly comfortable and warmer than normal stone.

Sinks offer a unique opportunity to customize your bathroom. Whether you are looking for a space-age, fluid bowl or a chunky, sturdy basin, sinks are available in every conceivable shape, size, and material. Glass sinks are clean and modern, although high-maintenance when it comes to cleaning as they show every watermark and fingerprint. Corian sinks are hard-wearing, like granite, but can be cast into any shape. Porcelain and ceramic basins are low-maintenance and versatile, perfectly at home in a country cottage or an urban loft. Be creative—you don't have to stick with a plain old pedestal. A simple ceramic bowl-shaped basin perched on a country-style table can work in a rustic or modern setting.

Make storage a priority in the bathroom, especially if you want to exploit the serenity of white fully. Unwanted clutter should be stowed out of sight, keeping surfaces clear and mess to a minimum. Invest in a bathroom cabinet to keep make-up orderly. Mirrored cupboards work well in small spaces since they double as storage. If you're fortunate to have a spacious bathroom, built-in concealed wall cabinets are a brilliant design feature,

THIS PAGE **An elegant Napoleonic-style cast-iron tub makes a fantastic centerpiece in an unusually spacious bathroom.** The romantic mood is given an edge with a vast, double-height mirror and stark, white wooden floorboards, which are practical as well as stylish. Touches of luxury abound, from the upholstered white stool piled with fresh towels to the elegant crystal candelabrum.

OPPOSITE, ABOVE LEFT AND RIGHT In a seaside home, a huge oval mirror maximizes light and space. The artful mix of an old-fashioned mirror with large, modern sink and streamlined faucets gives it character and individual style. The beachy bathroom has been painted shades of coffee and cream and given a relaxed feel with a driftwood-style paneled bathtub, and a retro, 1970s-style wicker chair to add a touch of glamour.

allowing masses of storage space for towels, linen, and toiletries. Keep your eyes open for unusual cupboards such as metal office cabinets or old gym lockers, which can be revamped by spray-painting them chalky white or gray. Or take a tip from kitchen design and use baskets on runners or simply place them on shelves under a sink. Otherwise redundant alcoves can house slatted shelves to store piles of fresh, fluffy towels, and antique French luggage rails with hooks can be used to stack baskets full of potions and lotions and to hang pretty washbags and washcloths.

Fixtures can make or break your bathroom, so be prepared to splurge on high-quality faucets and accessories, they will pull the whole look together and be functional and practical to boot. These days, you can buy amazing reproduction fixtures in the most humble of plumbing suppliers and builders' yards. There's also the option of hunting down reclaimed and restored faucets and accessories in salvage yards and at antique

ABOVE An antique French mirror painted white is a clever way to make a cramped bathroom feel and look roomier, while an old kitchen stool is used to display an orchid.

THIS PAGE The cool mix of stone and painted plaster, accessorized with a weathered Greek pot, gives this bathroom a Mediterranean feel. A round basin has been sunk into a limestone washstand, with faucets set into the wall to allow ample space for luxuries. Light is bounced around the room by a huge, circular mirror with beveled edges.

OPPOSITE Antique meets ultra-modern in this stylish urban bathroom. Sleek limestone contrasts with a decorative painted mirror and an ornate candelabrum. The smooth, curved washbasin appears to float on a polished stone surface.

BELOW LEFT **A roll-top tub is complemented by an old cream painted cupboard, which acts as storage for towels, linen, and toiletries.**

BELOW RIGHT **Old-fashioned fixtures are the perfect match for simple white utilitarian ceramic tiles.**

markets. If you really want to splash out, there are myriad designer faucets and shower fixtures, created to make your bathroom a high-performance haven. Faucets and showerheads can be set directly into the wall for a streamlined finish, minimizing the need to cover up obtrusive plumbing.

Bathrooms no longer have to be tiled from floor-to-ceiling. Tongue-and-groove is a perennial favorite. The perfect backdrop for a free-

THIS PAGE The multitonal concrete walls of this bathroom in a New York apartment are a surprising contrast to the elegant Art Deco bathtub and sink. A chrome mirror on a stand and a retro leatherette stool have a 1930s feel, while the elegantly draped shower curtain adds a touch of romance.

OPPOSITE, BELOW LEFT A walk-in shower is reminiscent of an old-fashioned public swimming baths. Painted turquoise walls are teamed with an aqua-colored glass shower screen and retro-style ceramic tiles laid in a brickwork pattern.

OPPOSITE, BELOW RIGHT Here, Ben de Lisi has used a square ceramic dish as a basin, which has been placed on a polished wood surface to create a chic, modern sink unit.

standing bathtub, it turns the plainest bathroom into a cozy sanctuary. Half-plastered, half-tiled walls look pristine and are easily maintained. Sparkling-white glazed tiles in a brick pattern have a retro, 1930s look not unlike public baths, while tiny glass or ceramic mosaic tiles can look ultra-modern or reminiscent of an old-fashioned lido pool, depending on the way they are used.

When it comes to painting walls, opt for specifically formulated bathroom paint, which will fare better in humidity, unless your bathroom is well ventilated. Highly polished plaster works well to create a Moroccan-style oasis, paired with flat finish, and slightly worn, terracotta tiles. Pick shades of white and off-white that are tranquil, such as stone, taupe, chalk, and lime white. Subtle accents of color such as watery blues and mint greens introduce a coastal element and delicate, faded pastels evoke a vintage mood.

What's underfoot is just as important as what is on the walls.

Bathroom floors tend to get constant wear and tear and are obviously vulnerable to water splashes and shampoo spills. Your first consideration should be safety, followed by practicality. Is it a non-slip surface? Will it be easy to clean? And is it water-resistant? Stone floors need not be ruled out; there are countless finishes available, such as rustic sandstone or hard-wearing industrial granite, both of which come in flat versions. You can experiment with materials and mix them together. Try juxtaposing hard-edged concrete with the organic feel of slatted wood, perfect for a bathroom with an open-plan shower area, or bring in a natural element with flat cobblestones set into concrete to create a border around the edges of the bathroom floor.

There's little need for excessive embellishment in a bathroom, apart from what you really need to bathe and beautify. Keep it simple with a beautiful potted purple Phalaenopsis orchid or a red Hibiscus rosa-sinensis for a dash of color.

ABOVE Unusual storage and vintage fixtures are one way to personalize a bathroom. The well-used weighing scales, found in an antique store, are a contrast to the shiny chrome basket, which provides storage for a bundle of fluffy, white towels.

OPPOSITE Tongue-and-groove paneling adds a Swedish feel to this bathroom. A simple console-style sink stand has the added benefit of a towel rod and a shelf to hold storage baskets, so the space is well-used. A Carl Larsson-inspired chair by Sasha Waddell provides comfortable seating, while a classical-style mirror reflects light back into the room. Privacy is maintained with a gauzy curtain hung up with café clips.

offices & workrooms

WHETHER IT'S A FULL-TIME OFFICE SPACE, A SEWING ROOM, OR
A STUDY, OFFICES HAVE BECOME PART AND PARCEL OF MODERN
HOMES. WITH TECHNOLOGY ON FAST FORWARD, WORKING FROM
HOME HAS NOW BECOME A REAL OPTION. WHILE YOU DON'T WANT
TO IMITATE THE DREARY, CORPORATE STYLE OF THE AVERAGE
WORKPLACE, DO TAKE ON BOARD SOME OF THE KEY ELEMENTS.
ORGANIZATION, STORAGE, COMFORT, AND LOCATION ARE CRUCIAL
CONSIDERATIONS. THERE'S NOTHING MORE DISTRACTING THAN
TRYING TO WORK IN A CLUTTERED, CHAOTIC ENVIRONMENT.
YOU CAN SQUEEZE AN OFFICE INTO ALMOST ANY SPACE—A CUBBY-
HOLE UNDER THE STAIRS, ON A LANDING, IN AN ATTIC, OR EVEN
AT THE END OF THE BACKYARD IN A SHED OR SUMMERHOUSE.
CONSIDER WHAT THE MAIN USE OF THE ROOM IS GOING TO BE. YOU
MIGHT NEED A ROOM FOR HOBBIES AND CRAFTING, A STUDY-
LIBRARY FOR FAMILY USE, AN OFFICE FROM WHICH TO RUN YOUR
BUSINESS, OR A PLACE WHERE YOU CAN DO YOUR ADMINISTRATION,
WRITE LETTERS, AND MAKE PHONE CALLS AWAY FROM THE HUBBUB
OF A BUSY HOME.

White, palest gray, and off-white are the ideal colors for a fuss- and clutter-free workroom. And, if color therapists are to be believed, a hint of baby blue or pastel green will be cooling and calming, while lilac white will stimulate creativity and help us to access our intuitive side.

Office walls don't have to be completely plain. Think about covering one wall with patterned wallpaper to make the space more homey and luxurious and to give work-weary eyes something to rest upon and contemplate.

If you tend to be a bit of a magpie and collect pages from magazines, photographs, and swatches of fabric, make a large bulletin board to display your collections. Cover a plain cork board with white felt, linen, or canvas and use it to pin up your clippings, then criss-cross it with bias binding or grosgrain ribbon.

If you have a self-contained workroom, opt for a floor that is practical and easy to sweep. White-painted boards, light-colored woods,

and polished concrete are all suitable treatments for a workroom floor. If you choose painted wood, make sure you have felted feet on all movable furniture to prevent scraping, and beware of chairs with castors, which can mark wood floors.

Good lighting is key, particularly for art and craft activities, so make it a priority. Make the most of natural daylight by positioning your desk next to or in front of a window. To control the amount of light streaming into your office, invest in Venetian blinds or louvered shutters. A desk lamp is essential when you are working in the evening or on a dreary day. Whether you choose a beautiful vintage 1930s desk lamp, a classic anglepoise, or ultra-chic Artemide lamp, invest in daylight simulation bulbs that radiate a light that is easy on the eye.

There's an old saying that "A tidy desk is a tidy mind," so make sure you choose a work table that you are going to be able to keep neat and tidy whilst allowing you the

ABOVE A glass vase makes practical storage for office bits and pieces.

OPPOSITE Patterned wallpaper adds a splash of femininity to this cool, modern workspace. A chrome and white leather chair, teamed with a retro desk lamp, a 1950s glass vase, and ashtray, takes it away from the dreariness of standard office furniture and accessories.

space to spread out materials and paperwork and accommodating a computer, telephone, and lamp. If you need a lot of space, think about building a desk or work-shelf that spans the entire width or length of your office. A basic desk can be easily constructed with a piece of heavyweight, shatterproof glass or laminated plywood and two decorator's trestle-tables. Even wallpaperer's tables painted pretty pastels or pure white can provide an ample work surface if budgets are an issue. If you don't have a designated office space, a built-in cupboard with a roll-down shutter, blind, or curtain is an excellent space-saver, allowing you to conceal your workspace when not in use.

Allow yourself a few touches of luxury. A bunch of fragrant, colorful sweet peas to soften the surroundings, a cactus to help absorb radiation from computers and electronic equipment, scented candles to make the room more tranquil and to alleviate stress, or a radio or i-Pod to play soothing or invigorating music when your nerves are frazzled or your energy levels are low.

TOP LEFT AND RIGHT **Feminine touches— fresh flowers, framed leaf pictures, and floral fabric—make these workspaces restful, stress-free environments.**

The owners of this Copenhagen
home have created a small but
light workroom using an old set
of glass doors they acquired in
exchange for a bottle of beer.
A trestle table, an antique chair,
and the original fixtures and beams
from the property's days as
a factory contrast with the
ultra-modern computer screen. A
collection of decorative gilt cherubs
and mirrors adds a whimsical
element to the office environment.

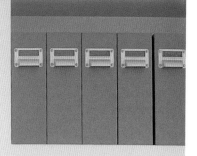

LEFT AND TOP RIGHT **Ample** shelving keeps this office functional, organized, and easy on the eye. Box files mean that paperwork and magazines can be stored in an orderly fashion. A double desk allows two people to work comfortably from home, while the courtyard garden beyond provides visual relief and a momentary escape from industry.

CENTER RIGHT **Classic Eames** rocking chairs provide comfortable seating in this spacious home office. A wall of clocks shows the time in different countries across the world.

BOTTOM RIGHT **A glass-top trestle** desk under a window means the owner of this home office is bathed in light while working. Glazed cabinets house a prolific magazine collection, so that everything is kept in order.

SOURCE DIRECTORY

US

ANTIQUES

English Country Antiques
Snake Hollow Road
Bridgehampton, NY 11932
(516) 537-0606
www.ecantiques.com
*Period country furniture
and decorative accessories.*

Highbrow Inc.
2110 8th Avenue South
Nashville, TN 37204
(888) 329-0219
www.highbrowfurniture.com
*Dealer of vintage modern
furniture, textiles, and
lighting.*

Moss
150 Greene Street
New York, NY 10012
(212) 204 7100
www.mossonline.com
*Original and reproduction
American decorative objects.*

Sage Street Antiques
Sage Street (off Route 114)
Sag Harbor, NY
(631) 725-4036
*Period furniture and
accessories.*

Therien and Company
716 North La Cienega
   Boulevard
Los Angeles, CA 90069
(310) 657-4615
www.therien.com
Period antique furniture.

Unica Home
7540 South Industrial
Road, Suite 501
Las Vegas, NV 89139-5965
(888) 89-UNICA
www.unicahome.com
*An impressive scope of
modern furniture and
accessories, both vintage
and reproductions, from
top designers.*

FURNITURE

Crate & Barrel
Visit www.crateandbarrel.com
to find a store near you.
*Clean, contemporary
furniture and accessories,
from simple white china
and glass to dining rooms
sets and beds.*

Design Within Reach
Visit www@dwr.com to
find a store near you.
*Provides access to well-
designed furnishings
traditionally found only
in designers showrooms. .*

Jenson-Lewis
89 Seventh Avenue
New York, NY 10011
(212) 929-4880
www.jensen-lewis.com
*A full selection of modern
home furnishings and
housewares.*

Pier One Imports
Visit www.pier1.com to
find a store near you.
*Home accessories,
furniture (indoor and out)
from all over the world.*

Pottery Barn
Call (800) 922-5507 or
visit www.potterybarn.com
to find a store near you.
*Pretty modern furniture and
accessories for the home.*

SALVAGE

Caravati's Inc.
104 East Second Street
Richmond, VA 23224
(804) 232-4175
www.caravatis.com
*Restoration materials and
architectural details from
old buildings.*

Florida Victorian
Architectural Antiques
112 West Georgia Avenue
Deland, FL 32724
(386) 734-9300
*Nineteenth- and early
twentieth-century
architectural elements.*

Salvage One
1840 West Hubbard
Chicago, IL 60622
(312) 733-0098
General salvage.

KITCHEN & BATHROOM

Kohler Co.
Call (800) 456-4537 or
visit www.kohlerco.com
for suppliers near you.
*Stylish hardware for
kitchen and bath.*

P. E. Guerin, Inc.
23 Jane Street
New York, NY 10014
(212) 243-5270
www.peguerin.com
Decorative hardware.

Restoration Hardware
Visit www.restorationhard
ware.com to find a store
near you.
*Fine hardware, home
furnishings, lighting, and
other accessories for the
home.*

Vintage Plumbing
9645 Sylvia Avenue
Northridge, CA 91324
(818) 772-1721
www.vintageplumbing.com
*Original and restored
to perfection bathroom
antiques, including pull-
chain toilets and clawfoot
bathtubs.*

Waterworks
23 West Putnam Avenue
Greenwich, CT 06830
(800) 998-BATH
www.waterworks.com
*Bathroom and kitchen
fixtures and fittings.*

TILES

Ann Sacks Tile & Stone
Visit www.annsacks.com
to find a stockist near you.
*High-quality selection of
tiles and stone surfaces.*

Country Floors
15 East Sixteenth Street
New York, NY 10003
(212) 627-8300
www.countryfloors.com
*Ceramics and terra-cotta
in the country style.*

Walker Zanger
8901 Bradley Avenue
Sun Valley, CA 91352
(818) 252-4000
www.walkerzanger.com
*Tiles in every material,
including metal and glass.*

LIGHTING

Ann Morris Antiques
239 East Sixtieth Street
New York, NY 10022
(212) 755-3308
www.annmorrisantiques
.com
*Fine reproduction lamps
and custom lamp shades.*

**Eron Johnson Antiques,
Ltd.**
451 North Broadway
Denver, CO 80203
(303) 777-8700
www.eronjohnsonantiques
.com
*Online retailer of antique
table lamps, wall sconces,
chandeliers, and more.*

Lampa + Möbler
6557 Costello Avenue
Valley Glen, CA 91401
(818) 634-4288
www.lampamobler.com
*Modernist and contemporary
light fixtures.*

Luis Baldinger & Sons, Inc.
www.baldinger.com
*Distributor of quality
lighting manufacturers.*

TEXTILES &
WALLPAPER

Gracious Home
1220 Third Avenue
New York, NY 10021
(212) 517-6300
www.gracioushome.com
*Bedding, linens, fine
fixtures, and other home
accessories.*

Portico Bed & Bath
www.porticohome.com
*Fine linens and luxury
beds.*

Thibaut
480 Frelinghuysen Avenue
Newark, NJ 07114
(800) 223-0704
*Textile dealer specializing
in wallpaper.*

Yves Delorme
Visit www.yvesdelorme
.com to find a stockist
near you.
*Sophisticated linens for
bed and bath.*

PAINT

Janovic
Visit www.janovic.com to
find a store near you.
*Quality paints from a wide
variety of makers.*

**Old Fashioned Milk Paint
Company**
436 Main Street
P.O. Box 222
Groton, MA 01450
(478) 448-6336
www.milkpaint.com
*Paints made from natural
pigments.*

**Pratt and Lambert
Historic Paints**
www.prattandlambert
.com
*150-year-old producer
of top of the line paints.*

UK

ANTIQUES

Glass etc.
18–22 Rope Walk
Rye TN31 7NA
andy@decanterman.com
01797 226600
Specialists in antique and 20th-century glassware.

Josephine Ryan Antiques
63 Abbeville Road
London SW4 9JW
020 8675 3900
www.josephineryanantiques
.co.uk
A haven of crystal chandeliers, antique mirrors, furniture and accessories. Also has a small range of elegant reproduction furniture.

Judy Greenwood Antiques
657–659 Fulham Road
London SW6 5PY
020 7736 6037
Antique beds, textiles and quilts along with a stunning selection of furniture and accessories from 18th century to the early 20th.

Pimpernel & Partners
596 King's Road
London SW6 2DX
020 731 2448
An eclectic mix of antique furniture, mirrors and decorative items.

SALVAGE & RECLAMATION

Lassco
30 Wandsworth Road
Vauxhall
London SW8 2LG
020 7394 2100
A salvage hunter's paradise filled with household fixtures and fittings.

Masco Walcot
Cirencester Road
Aston Down, Stroud
Gloucestershire GL6 8PE
01225 444404
www.walcot.com
Quality replicas, reclaimed flooring and oak beams, wooden panelling and bathroom fittings.

BATHROOMS

Alternative Plans
4 Hester Road
London SW11 4AN
020 7228 6460
One of the largest selections of limestone and stainless steel basins.

The Albion Bath Company Ltd
New Quay, Haven Road
Colchester C02 8HT
01206 794462
www.albionbathco.com
A wide range of cast-iron baths, modern and antique style sinks and washstands.

HOMEWARE

Atelier Abigail Ahern
137 Upper Street
London N1 1QP
020 7354 8181
www.atelierabigailahern.com
Everything from soft Merino wool blankets and recycled glass chandeliers to hand-thrown ceramics.

Brissi
Stores around London:
visit www.brissi.co.uk
A mix of painted furniture, and homeware with a Parisienne and New England feel.

Designers Guild
267–277 King's Road
London SW3 5EN
020 7351 5775
www.designersguild.com
Fabrics, wallpapers, furniture and accessories.

The Laundry
www.thelaundry.co.uk
Mail order company specialising in beautiful bedlinen and textiles.

The White Company
Call 0844 736 4222 or visit www.thewhitecompany.com to order or find a store near you.
Purveyors of the finest quality and predominantly white bedlinen, towels, home furnishings and accessories.

LIGHTING

London Lighting
135 Fulham Road
London SW3 5EN
020 7589 3612
www.londonlighting.co.uk
Designer lighting for every room in your home.

SKK
34 Lexington Street
London W1 3HR
020 7434 4095
Affordable modern lighting from a selection of young designers.

FURNITURE

Aria
Barnsbury Hall
Barnsbury Street
London N1 1PN
020 7704 6222
wwwariashop.co.uk
Modern Italian furniture and stockist of modern classics such as Verner Panton.

Chaplins
www.chaplins.co.uk
Modern furniture classics, lighting, flooring and accessories such as Vitra, Eames and B & B Italia.

Sasha Waddell Furniture
020 8979 9189
www.sashawaddellfurniture
.co.uk
Handcrafted furniture inspired by classic Swedish, French and east coast American designs.

SCP
135–138 Curtain Road
London EC2A 3BX
020 7739 1869
www.scp.co.uk
Contemporary English furniture and acessories by designers including Robin Day, Russell Pinch and Rachel Whiteread.

Viaduct
1–10 Summer's Street
London EC1R 5BD
020 728 8456
www.viaduct.co.uk
Modern classics and contemporary furnishings.

TILES

Bisazza
60 Sloane Avenue
London SW3 3DD
020 7584 8837
www.bisazza.com
Jewel-like mosaic tiles in every colour under the sun.

The Stone & Ceramic Warehouse
51–55 Stirling Road
London W3 8DJ
020 8993 5545
www.sacw.co.uk
Ho-style slate, stone and wenge-wood-look tiles.

TEXTILES & WALLPAPER

Cole and Son
Visit www.cole-and-son.com for a stockist near you.
Established in 1873, they have a huge array of traditional classics and up-to-the-minute wood block prints.

Colefax and Fowler
110 Fulham Road
London SW3 6HU
020 7244 7427
www.colefax.com
English wallpapers and fabrics featuring traditional as well as avant garde designs.

EW Moore & Son
39–43 Plashet Grove
London E6 1AD
020 8471 9392
www.ewmoore.com
Amazing selection of vintage wallpapers from the 1950s to the 1980s.

Marimekko
Visit www.marimekko.co.uk for a stockist near you.
Bold and bright Finnish fabrics and wallpapers.

Neisha Crosland
8 Elystan Street
London SW3 3NS
020 7584 7988
www.neishacrosland.com
Fabrics and wallpapers in an array of print-based designs.

Sandersons
01895 830044
www.sanderson-uk.com
English floral fabrics and wallpapers.

Voyage Decoration
www.voyagedecoration.com
Large range of charming fabrics.

KITCHENS

Bulthaup
37 Wigmore Street
London W1U 1PN
020 7495 3663
www.bulthaup.com
The crème de la crème of high-tech, super-sleek modern kitchens.

Plain English Kitchen Design
Stowupland
Stowmarket IP14 4BE
01449 774028
www.plainenglishdesign.co.uk
Simple, bespoke kitchens that work well in traditional or period settings.

FLOORING

Crucial Trading
www.crucial-trading.com
Natural floor coverings and rugs in hardwearing sisal, coir and sea grass.

The Natural Wood Flooring Company
www.naturalwoodfloor.co.uk
Huge collection of beautiful wood flooring.

PAINT

Farrow & Ball
Call 01202 876141 or visit www.farrow-ball.com for a stockist near you.
A huge range of whites, off-whites, and creams in traditional finishes.

The Paint Library
5 Elystan Street
London SW3 3NT
020 7590 9860
www.paintlibrary.co.uk
Premium quality paints and wallpapers that can be matched to any color scheme.

PICTURE CREDITS

ALL PHOTOGRAPHY BY POLLY WREFORD.
KEY: **a**=above, **b**=below, **r**=right, **l**=left, **c**=center

2 l London home of Michael Bains and Catherine Woram; **2 r** Siobhan McKeating's home in London; **3 l** Cecilia & Peter Granath's home in Copenhagen; **3 r** Harriet Maxwell Macdonald's home in London; **4 a & ac** Siobhan McKeating's home in London; **4 bc** Charlotte-Anne Fidler's home in London; **4 b** Cecilia and Peter Granath's home in Copenhagen; **5** Sasha Waddell's home available from www.beachstudios.co.uk; **6** Siobhan McKeating's home in London; **9** Ingrid & Avinash Persaud's home in London; **10** London home of Michael Bains and Catherine Woram; **12** Hilary Robertson and Alistair McCowan, Hastings; **14 l** Foster House at www.beachstudios.co.uk; **14 r** Siobhan McKeating's home in London; **15 l** Foster House at www.beachstudios.co.uk; **15 r & 16** Cecilia & Peter Granath's home in Copenhagen; **17 a, ac & b** Foster House at www.beachstudios.co.uk; **18** London home of Michael Bains and Catherine Woram; **20 al & br** Siobhan McKeating's home in London; **20 ar** Abigail Ahern's home in London; **20 bl & 22** Cecilia & Peter Granath's home in Copenhagen; **23 a, ac & bc** Foster House at www.beachstudios.co.uk; **23 b** Ben de Lisi's home in London; **24 al** Abigail Ahern's home in London; **24 ar** Ben de Lisi's home in London; **24 bl** Indenfor & Udenfor in Copenhagen; **24 br** Alex White; **26** Sasha Waddell's home available from www.beachstudios.co.uk; **27** Hilary Robertson and Alistair McCowan, Hastings; **28 al** Peri Wolfman & Charles Gold's New York loft; **28 ar** Harriet Maxwell Macdonald's home in London; **28 bl** Cecilia & Peter Granath's home in Copenhagen; **28 br** Charlotte-Anne Fidler's home in London; **30 & 31 b** Foster House at www.beachstudios.co.uk; **31a** Hilary Robertson and Alistair McCowan, Hastings; **32 al & br** Robert Levithan Residence, New York City; **32 ar & bl** Peri Wolfman & Charles Gold's New York loft; **34 al** London home of Michael Bains and Catherine Woram; **34 ar** Hilary Robertson and Alistair McCowan, Hastings; **34 b** Foster House at www.beachstudios.co.uk; **35** Robert Levithan Residence, New York City; **36 al** Ben de Lisi's home in London; **36 ar & bl** Foster House at www.beachstudios.co.uk; **36 br** Charlotte-Anne Fidler's home in London; **38–39** Sasha Waddell's home available from www.beachstudios.co.uk; **40** Siobhan McKeating's home in London; **43** Hilary Robertson and Alistair McCowan, Hastings; **44–45** Charlotte-Anne Fidler's home in London; **46–47** London home of Michael Bains and Catherine Woram; **46 inset** Hilary Robertson and Alistair McCowan, Hastings; **48–49** Hilary Robertson and Alistair McCowan, Hastings; **50** Cecilia & Peter Granath's home in Copenhagen; **51** Siobhan McKeating's home in London; **52** Foster House at www.beachstudios.co.uk; **53** Cecilia & Peter Granath's home in Copenhagen; **54 a & 55** Tom Fallon's house on Shelter Island; **55 b** Harriet Maxwell Macdonald's home in London; **56 l & 57** Tom Fallon's house on Shelter Island; **56 r** Foster House at www.beachstudios.co.uk; **58–59** Sasha Waddell's home available from www.beachstudios.co.uk; **60** Indenfor & Udenfor in Copenhagen; **61** Foster House at www.beachstudios.co.uk; **62–63** Sasha Waddell's home available from www.beachstudios.co.uk; **63 r & 65** Foster House at www.beachstudios.co.uk; **66–67** Abigail Ahern's home in London; **68–69** Robert Levithan Residence, New York City; **70–71** Alex White; **72** Foster House at www.beachstudios.co.uk; **74 al** Harriet Maxwell Macdonald's home in London; **74 ar** Siobhan McKeating's home in London; **74 bl** Hilary Robertson and Alistair McCowan, Hastings; **74 br**; Abigail Ahern's home in London; **76** www.susanchalom.com; **77** Harriet Maxwell Macdonald's home in London; **78–79** Siobhan McKeating's home in London; **80 a** Foster House at www.beachstudios.co.uk; **80 b & 81** Abigail Ahern's home in London; **82** Indenfor & Udenfor in Copenhagen; **83 a & bc** Foster House at www.beachstudios.co.uk; **83 ac** Robert Levithan Residence, New York City; **83 b** London home of Michael Bains and Catherine Woram; **84** Alex White; **85 l** Home of architect Reinhard Weiss & Bele Weiss in London; **85 r** Peri Wolfman & Charles Gold's New York loft; **86 a** Kathy Bruml's home in New Jersey; **86 bl** Cecilia & Peter Granath's home in Copenhagen; **86 br** Tom Fallon's house on Shelter Island; **87 & 88 al** Foster House at www.beachstudios.co.uk; **88 ar** Charlotte-Anne Fidler's home in London; **88 bl** Indenfor & Udenfor in Copenhagen; **88 br** Home of architect Reinhard Weiss & Bele Weiss in London; **90–91** Peri Wolfman & Charles Gold's New York loft; **92 l** Foster House at www.beachstudios.co.uk; **92 c** Charlotte-Anne Fidler's home in London; **92 r & 93** Siobhan McKeating's home in London; **94** London home of Michael Bains and Catherine Woram; **95** Home of architect Reinhard Weiss & Bele Weiss in London; **96–98 l** Foster House at www.beachstudios.co.uk; **98 r** Ben de Lisi's home in London; **99 l** Foster House at www.beachstudios.co.uk; **99 r** Home of architect Reinhard Weiss & Bele Weiss in London; **100–101** Abigail Ahern's home in London; **102** Indenfor & Udenfor in Copenhagen; **103** Foster House at www.beachstudios.co.uk; **103 inset** Sasha Waddell's home available from www.beachstudios.co.uk; **104 al** Tom Fallon's house on Shelter Island; **104 ar** Siobhan McKeating's home in London; **104 bl** Foster House at www.beachstudios.co.uk; **104 br** The Shelter Island home of Lois Draegin and David Cohen; **107** London home of Michael Bains and Catherine Woram; **108–111** Foster House at www.beachstudios.co.uk; **110 ar** Ingrid & Avinash Persaud's home in London; **112–113** Robert Levithan Residence, New York City; **114 b** Tom Fallon's house on Shelter Island; **114 al** The Shelter Island home of Lois Draegin and David Cohen; **114 ar & 115** Indenfor & Udenfor in Copenhagen; **116–117** Abigail Ahern's home in London; **118 al & bl** Foster House at www.beachstudios.co.uk; **118 ar** London home of Michael Bains and Catherine Woram; **118 br** The Shelter Island home of Lois Draegin and David Cohen; **120–121** Foster House at www.beachstudios.co.uk; **122** Siobhan McKeating's home in London; **123 a** Hilary Robertson and Alistair McCowan, Hastings; **123 b** Charlotte-Anne Fidler's home in London; **124** Abigail Ahern's home in London; **125** Siobhan McKeating's home in London; **126 a & bl** Indenfor & Udenfor in Copenhagen; **126 br** Ben de Lisi's home in London; **127** Alex White; **128** Sasha Waddell's home available from www.beachstudios.co.uk; **129–134** Foster House at www.beachstudios.co.uk; **134 b & 135** Indenfor & Udenfor in Copenhagen; **136–137** Ingrid & Avinash Persaud's home in London; **137 br** Charlotte-Anne Fidler's home in London; **141 a & bc** Abigail Ahern's home in London; **141 ac** Indenfor & Udenfor in Copenhagen; **141 b & 145** Foster House at www.beachstudios.co.uk.

ARCHITECTS & DESIGNERS WHOSE WORK IS FEATURED IN THIS BOOK:

Atlanta Bartlett
www.paleandinteresting.com

Atelier Abigail Ahern
137 Upper Street
London N1 1QP
020 7354 8181
020 7254 2299
contact@atelierbypost.com
www.atelierabigailahern.com
Pages 20 ar; 24 al; 66–67; 74br; 80 b; 81; 100–101; 116–117; 124; 141a & bc.

Beach Studios
01797 344077
01797 344044
office@beachstudios.co.uk
www.beachstudios.co.uk
Pages 14 l; 15 l; 17 a, ac & b; 23 a, ac & bc; 30; 31b; 34b; 36 ar & bl; 52; 56 r; 61; 63 r; 65; 72; 83 a & bc; 87; 88 al; 96; 98 l; 99 l; 103; 104 bl; 108–111; 118 al 7 bl; 120–121; 129–134 a; 141 b; 145.

Ben de Lisi
40 Elizabeth Street
London SW1 9NZ
020 7730 2994
020 7730 2881
bendelisi.com
Pages 23b; 24 ar; 98 r; 126 br.
Buy Ben de Lisi's bathroom and kitchen designs from:
ABACUS DIRECT LTD.
Abacus House
Jubilee Court
Copgrove
Harrogate HG3 3TB
0845 8505040
www.abacusdirectltd.com
Pages 98 r; 126 br.

Brissi Contemporary Living
196 Westbourne Grove
London W11 2RH
020 7727 2159
info@brissi.co.uk
www.brissi.co.uk
Pages 2 r; 20 al & br; 40; 74 ar; 92 r; 93; 122.

Granath
Pile Alle 53–55
2000 Frederiksberg
Copenhagen
Denmark
info@granath.com
www.granath.com
Pages 3 l; 4 b; 15 r; 16; 20 bl; 22; 28 bl; 50; 53; 86 bl.

Hilary Robertson
No. Eight
www.hilaryrobertson.com
and
Alistair McCowan
West Matravers
07770 765 106
al@westmatravers.com
Pages 27; 31 a; 34 ar; 43; 46 inset; 48–49; 74 bl; 123 a.

Indenfor & Udenfor antik
Toldbogade 65 B
DK-1253
Copenhagen K
Denmark
+45 22 34 94 53
www.indenfor.com
Pages 24 bl; 60; 82; 88 bl; 102; 114 ar; 115; 126 a & bl; 134 b; 135; 141 ac.

Kathy Bruml Homestyle
+212 645 1241
kathy@kathybruml.com
www.kathybruml.com
Page 86 a.

Michael Bains &
Catherine Woram
020 8672 3680
mbains@mac.com
catherine@cworam.demon.co.uk
www.catherineworam.co.uk
Pages 2 l; 10; 18; 34 bl; 46–47; 83 b; 94; 107; 118.

MMM Architects
The Banking Hall
26 Maida Vale
London W9 1RS
020 7286 9499
020 7286 9599
post@mmmarchitects.com
www.mmmarchitects.com
Pages 9; 110 ar; 136–137.

Ochre
020 7096 7372
enquiries@ochre.net
www.ochre.net
Pages 3 r; 28 ar; 55b; 74al; 77.

Susan Chalom
480 Park Avenue
New York, NY 10022
USA
+212 486 9207
susan@susanchalom.com
www.susanchalom.com
Page 76.

Peri Wolfman
Wolfman Gold
peri@charlesgold.com
Pages 28 al; 32 ar & bl; 85 r; 90–91.
Upholstered furniture available from:
MITCHELL GOLD
& BOB WILLIAMS
www.mgandbw.com

Reinhard Weiss
3s Architects and
Designers Ltd
172 Princes Road
Richmond
TW10 DQ
020 8332 9966
info@3s-ad.com
www.3s-ad.com
Pages 85 l; 88 br; 95; 99 r.

RL Design
+212 741 9762
rlevithan@earthlink.net
www.robertlevithan.com
and
Rudimar Kossman
Construction
+917 553 6151
Pages 32 al & br; 68–69; 83 ac; 112–113.

Sasha Waddell Interior
Design & Lectures
www.sashawaddelldesign.com
and
Sasha Waddell Furniture
Teed Interiors Ltd.
020 8979 9189
020 8979 0804
www.sashawaddell.co.uk
Pages 5; 26; 38–39; 58–59; 62–63; 103 inset; 128.

INDEX

Figures in italics indicate captions.

ACKNOWLEDGMENTS

First and foremost I would like to thank Polly Wreford for always taking such beautiful pictures no matter what. Her unfailing enthusiasm, creativity, and boundless energy are an inspiration. Thanks also to her two wonderful assistants, Miranda Swallow and Sarah Markillie for their hard work and support. Another huge thank you goes to Karena Callen for producing such enjoyable and inspiring text, not to mention keeping me laughing over cups of tea and the laptop. Thank you Karena. Lois Waldren, Georgie Lancaster and Katherine Mills cannot go unmentioned for their help and contributions in putting this book together as well as Mick Coote, Paul Burgess, Marcus Danka, and Robert Wilkes for pulling out all the stops when the chips were down. Thank you to my mother and of course everyone else who allowed us to photograph their gorgeous homes and to everyone at Ryland Peters & Small for their hard work and dedication, in particular Alison Starling, Miriam Hyslop, Pamela Daniels, and Jess Walton. Finally, on a personal note, thank you to my three beautiful sons for coping so well with my long absences and for all the kisses and cuddles on my return. Most of all thank you to my wonderful husband and soulmate, Dave, for everything.
Atlanta Bartlett

A massive thank you to Atlanta for giving me the opportunity to be part of this fantastic project – and for having faith in me – I have learned so much from you and have enjoyed it thoroughly; to Polly Wreford for the beautiful photography that has made this book such a visual pleasure to work on; to Pamela Daniels for her gorgeous layouts; and to Kate Mills for her invaluable help with research. In addition, a huge thank you to Miriam Hyslop for her guidance and support and generally being such a delight to work with. And last, but never least, thanks to my lovely family – Marty, Shannon, Scarlet, and Tilly – for putting up with my working night and day. As you can see, it was worth it!
Karena Callen